SHIRTS
MERICAN
ON
DANIEL DeWEESE

1919

Miller & Co. established as first Western wholesale jobber

....

1923

Stockman-Farmer Catalog published, the first in the Western-wear business

....

1930s

Early transitional sportswear/ Western shirts made with buttons

1946

Rockmount Ranch Wear established; makes the first com- mercially made snap shirts, eventually becoming the longest- running brand

1946

Westmoor established as a sportswear maker; later produces Western snap shirts

1948

Karman established

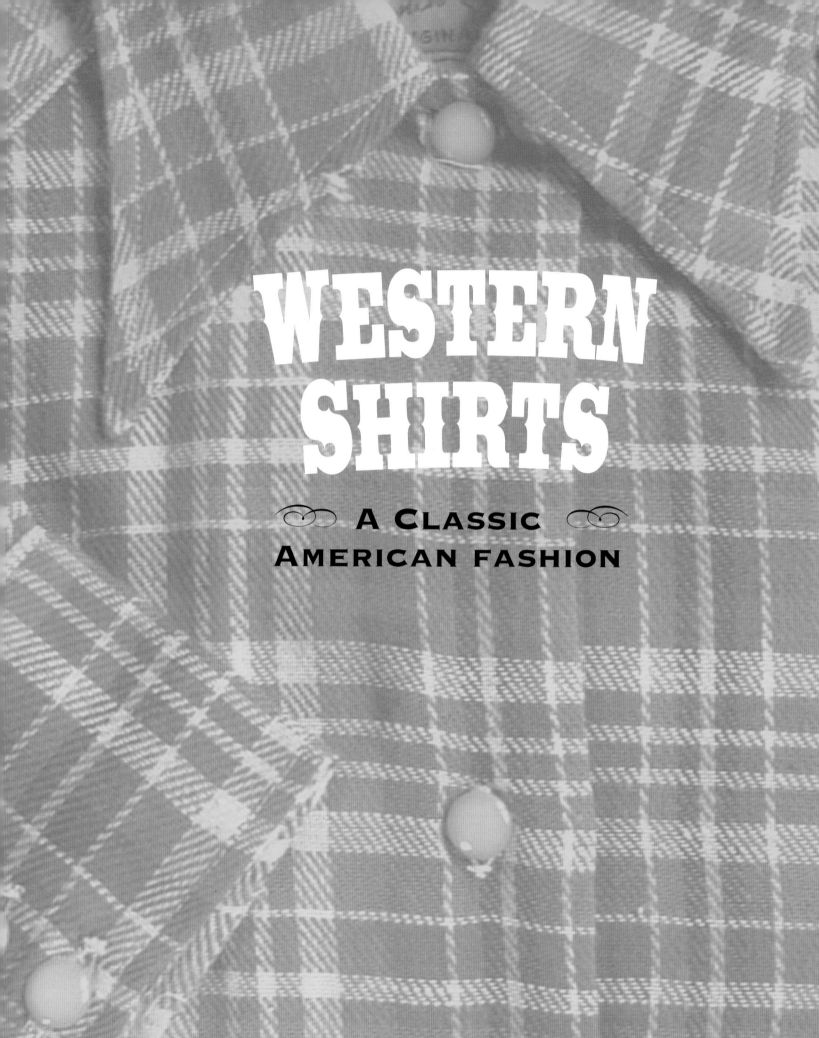

WESTERN SHIRTS

A Classic
American fashion

WESTERN SHIRTS

A CLASSIC AMERICAN FASHION

STEVEN E. WEIL AND G. DANIEL DeWEESE

PHOTOGRAPHS BY
STEVEN E. WEIL

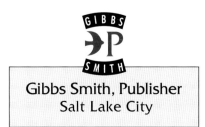

Gibbs Smith, Publisher
Salt Lake City

First Edition

08 07 06 05 04   5 4 3 2 1

Text © 2004 Steven E. Weil and G. Daniel DeWeese

Photographs © 2004 Steven E. Weil, except where noted

Published by

Gibbs Smith, Publisher

P.O. Box 667

Layton, Utah 84041

Orders: 1.800.748.5439

www.gibbs-smith.com

Designed by Tom Sieu

Printed in Hong Kong

Library of Congress Cataloging-in-Publication Data

DeWeese, G. Daniel

  Western shirts : a classic American fashion / G. Daniel DeWeese and Steven E.

Weil.— 1st ed.

     p. cm.

  Includes bibliographical references.

  ISBN 1-58685-248-5

  1. Shirts, Men's—West (U.S.) 2. Shirts, Men's—Collectors and

collecting. 3. Cowboys—Clothing—West (U.S.) I. Weil, Steve. II.

Title.

TT612.D48 2004

391'.046362'13092—dc22

                          2004008599

Image opposite title page: Ben The Rodeo Tailor, Philadelphia. Men's two-tone, heavy gabardine, 1940s. This shirt, created by one of the great, early cowboy tailors, features special scallop shotgun cuffs, downward-pointing smile pockets, contoured yokes with soutache outline, enamel snaps, a reinforced collar band, and straight tails with deep side scoops. Courtesy of Cowboy Story Land & Cattle Co., Cody, Wyoming.

★ ★

DEDICATION

This book is dedicated to my grandfather Jack A. Weil, without whom there would be no book, possibly no subject for it. Papa Jack was not only "there when it happened," he was critical to the advent and popularization of Western wear.

His life has spanned a century and touched thousands; his impact has truly reached millions—we hear from people across the globe who wear and live Western clothes. But the numbers don't tell the whole story. Though Papa Jack designed, produced, and sold some of the first commercially made Western shirts, his legacy is much more than just textiles. He has imparted a way of life, and the thousands of people he has met in his long life—helped start in business, clothed, or just shared his story with—all share in common the notion that they are better off for it.

When I started at Rockmount Ranch Wear in 1981 and then applied for a credit card, I asked him what I should say for length of employment—I had grown up in the business. His reply never left me: "If you tell the truth you never have to remember what you said."

When he moved to Denver from Indiana as a young man in 1926, he brought with him honesty and a respect for individuals. He shows the same respect talking to the mayor or a corporate president as he does to the trucker who just delivered the last shipment. His integrity is rock solid and his word is his bond.

Jack Weil has given people everywhere a bit of himself that he treasures—the West—because as he says, "The West is not a place, it is a state of mind."

—Steven E. Weil

Jack A. Weil on the occasion of his 103rd birthday.
Photo by Paul Trantow.

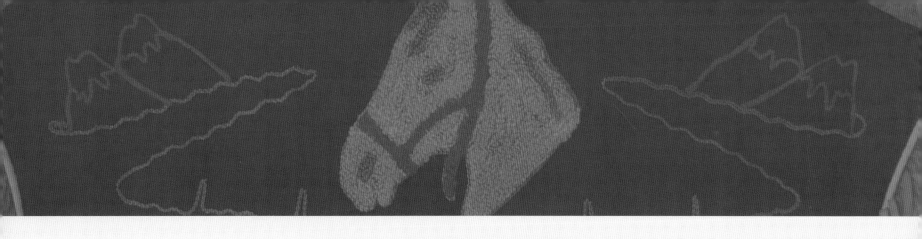

CONTENTS

PREFACE   8

ACKNOWLEDGMENTS   10

INTRODUCTION   12

PART 1:   THE SHIRT
          Chapter 1: A History of Western Shirts   19
          Chapter 2: Vintage Shirts as Collectibles   26
          Chapter 3: Design Elements of Western Shirts   34

PART 2:   THE MANUFACTURERS
          Chapter 4: Miller Western Wear   67
          Chapter 5: Rockmount Ranch Wear Mfg. Co.   79
          Chapter 6: The H Bar C Story   88
          Chapter 7: Levi Strauss & Co.   98
          Chapter 8: The Karman, Inc. Story   107
          Chapter 9: The Westmoor Story   116
          Chapter 10: Significant Others   125

PART 3:   THE LABELS
          Chapter 11: Western Shirt Labels   135

PART 4:   APPENDIX
          Glossary   163
          Bibliography   168
          Resources   169

★ ★

"I LOVE YOUR DESIGNS AND WISH YOU WELL FOR THE NEXT MILLION YEARS . . ."

—E-MAIL TO ROCKMOUNT FROM LYNN SIEFERT, AGUA DULCE, CALIFORNIA

T he perpetual demand for vintage Western shirts, since they were new through present day—more than seventy years, establishes the apparel as a true fashion classic. Western shirts are also one of the few original American fashions. While there are older traditions in American fashion—for example, the trade blankets worn 150 years ago by American Indians—few, if any, have been worn with the continuity of Western shirts. There was a time when old Indian saddle blankets were as utilitarian, common, and inexpensive as Western shirts. Today, both are serious collectibles whose values are rising.

There is a deeply rooted appreciation of the Western shirt as part of true Americana. It is not a "dead language" to be studied only in books and museums. These shirts remain on the street, vibrant and popular worldwide.

The hunt is half the fun; finding a really great piece is the payoff. People occasionally bring me vintage Rockmount Ranch Wear, as they know it is my passion. One time a former Rockmount retailer from Indiana dropped off a beautiful men's shirt made of Egyptian cotton, a fine fabric then and now. It had hex snaps from the 1950s and still had original folding. The shirt escaped being sold for cheap when he liquidated; he had kept it for its intrinsic value out of respect. When he heard that I collect vintage Rockmount, he passed it on to me for safekeeping. It was my size and I thought about wearing it, but in the end I could not bring myself to do it; it seemed sacrilegious to let a piece of history be defaced with a splash of coffee. The fact that it had survived in new condition for more than fifty years meant it deserved to be preserved.

While my interest in scouring vintage stores for cool Western shirts is just a step away from my father's higher pursuit of early-American antiques, my crazy hobby is far cheaper. My own collection was partly inspired by visits as a teenager to my grandfather Papa Jack's closet. There is something to be said for a family with plenty of storage space and a resistance to discarding things as they age. Years later, having exhausted the family's Rockmount warehouse in search of old classics, I stopped at every vintage store I passed on business and personal travels across the country. Later, I expanded the search even further to Europe and Japan, where there is a special appreciation for Americana. For me, this chance to see and feel history rivaled a visit to the Louvre or the Museum of Modern Art.

★ ★

My pursuit of vintage Western is largely motivated by an interest in the family legacy. For twenty years I have been hanging great old Rockmount pieces in the company's lobby museum. As each piece comes into my world, I record its provenance and archive its story, adding whatever history my grandfather and father can remember upon seeing a shirt they made fifty or sixty years ago. It is amazing to me how, despite the decades, my 103-year-old grandfather's photographic memory can instantly recall a fascinating bit of history on what inspired the make of a given shirt, its fabric, or a production detail.

Not only does Rockmount have a lot of history, it is headquartered in a historic landmark building located in Denver's historic Lower Downtown district, "LoDo." We have a constant stream of people coming through the door. They peruse the vintage collection in the lobby with wonderment.

Then in 2000, I met Gibbs Smith, a man with a fondness for making the world a better place through books. Until then it had never occurred to me that preserving this history, which has personal meaning to me, would ever be as interesting to others.

Over the years and especially while preparing this book, I have come to know many others who collect and appreciate original Western shirts as art. Who better to join me in introducing this labor of love, than my friend of twenty years, Dan DeWeese, a veteran editor of Western trade magazines? His many years as a commentator on the Western apparel industry gives this book a unique perspective. It took a special rapport to gain access to the company principals, who are otherwise private, as we reconstructed this history from a wide range of sources.

The time is ripe for the first book focused entirely on vintage Western shirts. This book honors those who contributed to the popularity of Western shirts, the manufacturers who made them, the stores that sold them, those who wore them, and the crazy people like me who collect them. Lynn, whether you're a collector, historian, or simply someone who enjoys the unique beauty and workmanship from a golden era of Americana, this is the best way I know to keep this going for the next million years.

—Steven E. Weil

Rockmount Ranch Wear, men's rayon gabardine with embroidery soutache. The brown, enamel cap snaps predate pearl snaps; the Bakelite shank button at the collar is a holdover predating snaps. The Celanese "Flannese" fabric, with special tail label, has the look of wool gabardine but is lighter for year-round wear. The slim-fit size stamp in the collar band marked "convertible collar" predates size tags. The shirt features smile pockets, tail gussets, and sportswear-like double pleats on the back. Courtesy of Rockmount, Denver, Colorado.

★ ★ ★ ★ ★ ★   ★ ★ ★ ★ ★ ★

Acknowledgments

There would be no book were there no shirts. So many people contributed to the advent and perpetuation of Western fashion that it is impossible to acknowledge all. At its most abstract, the Western lifestyle is the inspiration that led people like the Weils, Millers, Christenfelds, Hochsters, and Mandelbaums to devote their careers to it. When the nature of fashion is that it comes and goes, why has Western fashion remained popular for seventy years?

When you think about the people who live the Western life and wear the clothes, work in the companies that design them, the factories that make them, the stores that sell them and all the related businesses such as the media, trade shows, and the raw-materials suppliers, it is inconceivable how many people contribute to what this is all about. Suffice it to say millions. In writing this book it is our hope to uncover their stories and help preserve these icons of American culture.

We would like to give special thanks to:

Jack A. and Jack B. Weil, for creating a family legacy and passing it on to the rest of us;

Wendy Weil and Julie Thorndycraft, for supporting our effort to write this book and not sparing our feelings when a reality check was needed;

Colter Weil, the future, for his huge love of books despite his few years;

Gibbs Smith, our publisher who gave Steven the idea for the book, then made it a reality. Also, our editors Suzanne Taylor and Johanna Buchert Smith for giving it life;

Ronnie Weiser, devoted collector and true vintage Western maniac, who made his incredible collection available;

Katy Kattelman, Katy K. of Ranch Dressing in Nashville, who helped source the materials from the Rockmount Vintage Collection and promotes the look through her vision;

Dan Shapiro, Southwest, Ltd. Vintage Western Wear, holder of the flame for H Bar C, who generously shared his archive and collection;

The many vintage stores we visited in the United States and abroad that let us research shirts and labels;

★ ★

The museums that recognize the art in vintage Western and legitimize collecting it as an art form, and who helped our research: the Gene Autry Museum of Western Heritage, the National Cowboy and Western Heritage Museum; the Buffalo Bill Historic Center, and the Cowgirl Hall of Fame;

Seymour Simmons, retired chairman, and Ron Schmitz, president, of Miller International (formerly Miller & Co.), which published the first Western catalog, Stockman-Farmer Supply. Ron kindly made available the company's catalog archive, a fascinating glimpse into how Western fashion evolved;

Don Reeves, curator at the National Cowboy and Western Heritage Museum, who let Steven into the inner sanctum where they store the cool stuff;

Nobu Hirota of Cactus Blues, Steve's guide in Japan to so many vintage stores he would never have found by himself. Also, Nobu deserves credit for recognizing the intrinsic beauty of contemporary classic Western design and bringing it to Japan;

Lynn Downey, historian at Levi Strauss & Company;

Jerry Glick and Ruth Ann Hattori, for assisting with the information about Prior;

Gary Mandlebaum, president of Karman, Inc., maker of Roper;

Jeff Hochster, president of Westmoor, Inc., maker of Panhandle Slim;

Bill Hervey and Joe Hertz at VF Corporation, maker of Wrangler;

Steven L. Wright of The Winthrop Group, Inc., archivist/historian for Pendleton Woolen Mills;

Alan and Mike Luskey, the third generation to run the Luskey Stores in Texas, for making available catalogs from the '50s and '60s;

David "LeRoy" Heimermann for digitizing much of the historical material.

★ ★

My interest in vintage Rockmount arose as a teenager. I loved the shirts in my grandfather's closet, ones he had made in the 1940s and '50s. I absconded with some—and learned why you never wash and dry woolen gabardine. My desire to preserve history by hanging Papa Jack's shirts in our lobby museum ran counter to his desire to stay warm; on cold Colorado winter days, he would take my exhibits home to wear. For him they were meant to be worn; for me, to preserve.

While working part-time during high school at Rockmount's warehouse, I found a couple of very early shirts. Vintage Western wear did not yet have cachet in the 1970s, but I safeguarded these great old pieces anyway.

Rockmount Ranch Wear women's two-tone gabardine with embroidery, 1940s. This early example of women's Western fashion has all the classic design elements: tailored fit, two-tone styling, embroidery, and snaps. The black enamel cap-snap fasteners predate pearl snaps. The black Bakelite shank button at the collar predates snaps. Made of Celanese "Flannese" fabric, with a special tail label, this shirt has the look of wool gabardine but is lighter for year-round wear. It also has many sportswear features including French-front lapels, a sport collar, side seam vents at the tail, and stylized built in slash pockets. Courtesy of Rockmount, Denver, Colorado.

Collecting vintage Western wear was a bizarre idea when Larry McMurtry wrote *Cadillac Jack* in 1982, the story of an itinerant rare-antiquities dealer with a penchant for vintage cowboy boots. I had never heard of anyone who really collected vintage Western wear back then.

When I returned to Denver in 1981 after college and graduate school, I remembered the cool old shirts I had put in safekeeping. I searched periodically throughout our 30,000-square-foot office and warehouse. I finally found the early shirts in an old desk that had been moved to the basement. Eureka! By this time vintage collecting was popular on the coasts and beginning to gain a foothold more widely. I framed the old shirts, hung them in the lobby, and began buying back special Rockmount pieces found during my travels. My grandfather thought I was crazy.

Everyone has a story about their favorite find. On a 1985 trip to Los Angeles, I found a store on Melrose Street that had just one old Western shirt, hung high over the transom above the door. The store owner wanted to bring it down for me to see. "Thanks anyway," I said. "I only look for Rockmount." When a brand is in your blood you figure you can smell it from across the street.

He said, "Take a look anyway," and took it down. I did not recognize the make—a brown gabardine with soutache embroidery everywhere (see page 9). My heart nearly stopped when I saw the rainbow label. It predated any Rockmount shirt I had ever seen, which is why I had not recognized it. Its enameled snaps were the first I had ever seen. It was priced at seventy dollars. In 1985, our new shirts were

Rockmount Ranch Wear, women's sleeveless shirt, 1954. This is one of Jack B. Weil's early designs. Very stylized, this rayon shirt features diamond snaps, saddle stitching, rare double-pointed pocket flaps, shoulder and tail vents, and double-needle side seams. It retains a sportswear influence with its French-front lapels and sport collar. Courtesy of Rockmount, Denver, Colorado.

generally thirty dollars. I told the retailer that my grandfather had designed the shirt when he started the company. Touched, he said, "Take the shirt, send me a couple new ones."

Excited, I hurriedly called my grandfather from a pay phone on the street. Incredulous, he said, "*What!* You *traded* two perfectly good new shirts for an old one we sold for three dollars forty years ago? We sold it once, why would you buy it back?"

That old brown shirt inspired me to start designing. Remaking it was a challenge that taught me how to design. I also reinterpreted some others of my grandfather's and father's original designs. Like the patterns, none of the fabrics or treatments had been in use for decades. It was a wheel that had to be reinvented. That was eighteen years ago. The Vintage Collection is now an ongoing part of our line. We do not simply remake these vintage pieces when we find a good one that we have not seen in decades. We have to practically reinvent it. And although we are constantly

★ ★

on the prowl for truly great classics, they are hard to come by (which is why they are collectible). Sure we use a contemporary fit, new fabrics, and new colors, but the inspiration is clearly classic. We created a new market for classic Western fashion and had it largely to ourselves until recently; now many other brands have followed. By the way, I see the vintage guy once in awhile at M.A.G.I.C., the largest men's apparel show. He recently said the old brown shirt is now worth $600. I'm lucky I got it. I have never seen another.

Originals were fairly easy to find in thrift and vintage stores until the early 1990s, and did not cost much. Today, the good ones never reach thrift store sales floors. Professional pickers route them to higher-end vintage stores at home and abroad. Better pieces from the 1950s and earlier are priced at more than $200. The once-abundant supply of pre-1960s vintage clothing has finally been nearly exhausted. Good pieces continue to surface but they are expensive and rare. The value of good vintage, like all better antiques, appreciates with time. The great shirts from the 1940s and '50s that used to be hung on the racks are now displayed on the wall. The good ones go out of circulation, which is why this book is needed to document them.

As time goes by, it becomes more difficult to reconstruct the history of Western shirts. Many of the early brands are gone. Those still in business seldom maintained archives; their mission was to sell, not warehouse. However, Miller, Levi Strauss & Co., and Rockmount had the foresight to maintain archives. Miller has maintained its catalogs since the 1930s. Levi Strauss & Co. has a historian. Rockmount has an extensive shirt collection. The other material for this book had to be researched far and wide. Finding it in vintage stores and collections was serendipity; a comprehensive historical archive does not exist. Dan and I agreed, however, it would be better to show just the highlights than show nothing at all. This survey of makers and their designs comes from a wide range of sources. Some brands remain in business, but the history of Western shirts has been drying up over the decades as companies close and their principals pass away. A number of museums have a collection of vintage shirts and photographs of people wearing them: the National Cowboy and Western Heritage Museum; the Museum of the America West, formerly known as Autry Museum; the National Cowgirl Museum and Hall of Fame; and others are dedicated to preserving Western history. Vintage stores around the world actually have the widest collections, but their shirts disperse quickly. It is the private collections of vintage collectors that actually give us the most comprehensive look at brands and styles over the years.

We credit other works in our bibliography, though these generally cover Western wear as a whole without much focus on shirts themselves.

★ ★

STOCKMAN-FARMER

SUPPLY COMPANY
1929-1933 LAWRENCE ST.
DENVER · COLORADO

MILLER
WESTERN WEAR

CATALOG 49 FALL AND WINTER 1936-37

This catalog was designed by Jack A. Weil while a partner at Miller & Co. Jack brought the Miller catalog business into the modern age with the first four-color catalog in the Western business. The other major Western catalogs in the 1930s, such as Porter's of Phoenix (see their shirt label in chapter 11) and Hamley's of Pendleton, were all black and white. Jack's mission was about popularizing the romance of the West. His catalog covers were based on paintings by leading Western artists. His agreement with the artists included publishing prints, too. During the Great Depression they sold hundreds of thousands of Western prints at twenty-five to thirty-five cents each. Courtesy of Jack A. Weil, Denver, Colorado.

The photos of shirts and labels have primarily come from my travels across the United States, Japan, and Europe, where I have visited more than fifty vintage stores. Every store has offered a treasure, often an unsung brand that I had never seen previously.

The nature of this subject is somewhat elusive. As a collector for over thirty years, I find that one rarely sees good early pieces for sale. During this pursuit of great old Rockmounts, I have found only eight prime early examples. Three of these survived because they were lost between the cracks in the company warehouse.

Fashion trends are based on the bromide: out with the old, in with the new. The beauty of classic style, however, is that it does not bounce around like a ping-pong ball from season to season. Western shirts were meant to be worn; keeping them for posterity seems contrary to their purpose. People like their favorite shirts so much, they wear them to threads. Rockmount receives so many requests to patch a shirt purchased ten or twenty years ago that it no longer surprises us. The joke is that we wished we had one hundred customers like them, not thousands. But it is a testament to the integrity of the shirts, the intrinsic quality of their design, workmanship, and materials, that they remain for us to enjoy for forty, fifty, sixty years.

We have documented over 135 different brands on the market from the last seventy years, with an estimated combined production of hundreds of millions of Western shirts. Yet, relatively few of the older ones remain in the secondary market for us to document. Vintage Western shirts are victims of their own popularity. Our research is complicated by the exodus of Western collectibles to Europe and Japan. The foreign market began collecting them earlier and more aggressively than the domestic market because they recognized the historical value of intrinsic Americana ahead of its native country. Once exported, as I have seen in Japan, they are prohibitively expensive to reacquire; better pieces average two hundred dollars.

— Steven E. Weil

Below: Rockmount Ranch Wear, men's rayon print, 1940s. This is the earliest Western print we have seen. With obvious similarities to Hawaiian-print shirts, it has a motif which comes from cowboy scarves of the same era, with every Western scene in a cloud. It seems contemporary but close inspection reveals design elements from the 1940s: a contoured collar with removable stays, early yellow synthetic snaps, and felled side seams with tail gussets. Courtesy of Kay Iverson, Florida.

The goal of this book is to preserve a little piece of American Western history. The period covered is the first fifty years of Western shirts, from the 1930s to the 1980s. Western shirt design flowered into a Golden Age during the 1940s to the 1960s, our focus. This is the key period when shirt design exploded in unsurpassed creativity, artistry, and special treatments. The brands featured are those that played significant roles in building the Western shirt market. The shirts documented are those that are especially collectible. Our concern is mostly with history and design. The label guide, on the other hand, features as many brands as possible to show the incredible range produced over the years. Shirt values are not listed because they are subjective and variable.

It was a labor of love to survey this long-lived subject and trace its early days, and those who laid the groundwork for all that followed. Now, let's look at what made Western shirts popular in the first place.

★ ★

★ ★ ★ ★ ★ ★ ★ ★ ★ ★ ★ ★ ★ ★ ★ ★ **PART 1** ★ ★ ★ ★ ★ ★ ★ ★ ★ ★ ★ ★ ★ ★ ★ ★

The Shirt

CHAPTER 1

★

⚮ A HISTORY OF ⚭

WESTERN SHIRTS

Western wear began as a costume but became part of a lifestyle. The early rodeo cowboys and actors in Western movies wore custom-made costumes. These clothes were fashioned by tailors or were homemade. The most famous tailors—Turk, Sing Kee, Rodeo Ben, Nudie, Fay Ward, and others—were genuine artists who sparked the creation of Western design, but their output and reach were limited. Their suits and shirts, though ornate and constructed with intricate detail, were flashy to the point of kitsch. They also only made one piece at a time and charged plenty for it. After all, they were tailors to the day's cowboy movie stars, the first entertainers with mass appeal.

In order to understand how Western fashion became popular, it should be put in the context of popular culture. The West was first popularized by dime novels. Billions of them were published during a fifty-year period beginning in 1860, according to the Buffalo Bill Museum in Golden, Colorado. This was the first mass-produced entertainment industry, something like the television of its day. Dime novels fed the myth of the West to the hero-starved East. The Wild West shows of Buffalo Bill and the Miller Brothers' 101 Ranch took the West on the road, thrilling audiences across the United States of America and Europe. Silent films, and later "talkies," took off where the Wild West shows had left off, perpetuating the romance and excitement of the West.

Dude ranches also played an important role in spreading the word. Eastern tourists began visiting the West by train during the last quarter of the nineteenth century and have been going ever since. The term "dude" may actually have as its origin a disparaging comment on the "duds" worn by city slickers pretending to be cowboys.

Harris Tailoring Co., Fort Worth, Texas. Men's two-tone gabardine with embroidery and piping. Courtesy of the National Cowboy and Western Heritage Museum, Oklahoma City, Oklahoma.

The Emergence of the Western Business

The public had a thirst for Western wear that the high-end tailors could not quench. Working cowboys and guests at dude ranches liked what they saw at the rodeos and on the silver screen. Phil Miller, the first Western-wear jobber, founded Miller & Co. in Denver in the 1920s. He meant to satisfy the public's emerging desire for all things Western. Jack A. Weil joined him in 1933 and developed what is believed to be the first Western shirt manufacturing business. Jack A. recalls studying the custom outfits worn in the movies during the 1930s. They influenced his designs. After World War II, he founded Rockmount Ranch Wear.

About the same time, the Christenfelds of H Bar C, Sam Mandelbaum of Karman, Ernest Hochster of Westmoor, and others started making Western shirts. These were the brands that dressed the West. H Bar C was originally a New York pants maker that later opened a West Coast office and went into the Western shirt business. Karman arose from Denver's Miller & Co. Westmoor was a midwestern sportswear manufacturer that went into Western shirts later.

While the movies captured the public's imagination, dude ranches helped facilitate the spread of Western fashion after World War II. When Easterners visited dude ranches, they took Western garb home. It was a novelty not sold where they lived. This was instrumental in spreading the culture of the American West. Ironically, American history is often characterized by the East moving West, but in this case, Western wear went the other way and kept on going.

The genius of the early manufacturers was that they created and then supplied a market for Western shirts. They innovated production techniques to produce the new fashion, and it proved to be an enduring one: many of the styling and design treatments created by the cowboy tailors and the early factory-shirt designers changed little for almost forty years. This could not have been accomplished by a few tailors making custom garments for show people. Commercial production is what spread the fashion and dressed a culture. The various companies were small but produced distinctive, high-quality clothes, with all kinds of special treatments for a niche market, and they launched the golden age of Western wear.

The Western apparel industry had relatively steady growth from the 1930s through the 1970s. At first, both the market and the industry were geographically situated out West. Department stores, tack stores, feed stores, and boot-repair shops would take on some Western items. If they sold, they would expand their stock of Western wear. This process had spread eastward by the 1950s. By 1970, there were about 1,000 stores selling Western shirts.

The Urban Cowboy

In 1978, it all suddenly changed. Once again, Western attire got a boost from the silver screen. The movie *Urban Cowboy*, starring John Travolta, fanned a wildfire that catapulted Western wear from the niche market to the mass market for the first time. The number of stores carrying Western shirts shot from a thousand to several thousand. Big-name designers "discovered it" and brought Western style from the country to the city. Western companies could sell everything they could make and increased production to meet the demand. New suppliers flocked to the market. A lot of wild, flamboyant styles were made for the new Westerners, such as the satin, two-toned shirt Travolta wore in the movie.

It was a buoyant time, but the fashion business never stands still. The Urban Cowboy proved to be a bubble that burst the Western industry's forty-plus years of steady growth. The industry suffered its first significant downturn in 1981. People in the industry thought the boom would never end, but, just like the nineteenth-century gold rushes, it was followed by a bust. The aftermath of the Urban Cowboy bust was far reaching and long lasting. Hundreds of stores closed; many Western brands never recovered. Some manufacturers were consolidated, others, such as Stetson, went bankrupt. When the sales spike ended in 1981, it was if somebody had shut off the water. Those that survived had not bet the ranch on the Urban Cowboy. They still had a core market, and once the dust settled, sales returned to pre–Urban Cowboy levels.

> **The genius of the early manufacturers was that they created and then supplied a market for Western shirts, innovating styling and design treatments that changed little for almost forty years.**

When the Urban Cowboy fad ended in 1981, the core Western market reacted against flamboyant Western styling. Ironically, the Urban Cowboy, a highly stylized look, almost killed Western fashion, which gave way to conventional design with little or no Western styling. Gone in many lines were the special treatments that are intrinsic to Western design. The post–Urban Cowboy look of most brands was "crossover," a blend of conventional and Western looks. The 1980s and '90s were almost entirely characterized as hybrid knockoffs of mainstream fashion designer looks, with color blocking, single patch pockets, and no front yokes or snaps. This trend continued until 2003 when most Western brands went retro.

The next boom arrived with the twang of country music and the stomp of line dancers, a decade after the Urban Cowboy went suburban. Before line dancing declined in the mid-1990s and took Western shirt sales down with it, new clubs opened across North America, Europe, and Asia. Combined with other factors, this boom and bust cycle caused another large industry fallout. Again, hundreds of Western stores closed.

Western Shirts and General Fashion: The Tide Goes Both Ways

There is a natural ebb and flow to the tides of style, whether it is an art movement or a fashion trend. Sometimes the fashion trend is an organic development and sometimes a less-innocent, wholesale rip-off. Originally, as Western shirts developed into a new fashion genre, they were strongly inspired by sportswear. General fashion trends in fabrics and colors have always played a strong role in Western shirt design over the years, if for no other reason than the early fabrics and colors available to Western-shirt makers were the same found in mainstream categories. There was a sportswear influence from the 1930s through the early 1950s. While the Western shirt was deeply influenced by prevailing trends in its early years, the favor would later be returned in a huge way. Mainstream fashion first accepted Western shirt styling as a fashion category in the late 1970s.

Western design went through a transitional period when it took baby steps away from conventional fashion. It took many years before Western evolved into a completely separate stylistic direction. Looking at the contoured collars, French fronts, back pleats, and flap pockets that characterize Western from the 1930s–1950s, it is easy to see how it sprang from this popular look in general fashion.

As Western design gained momentum, it developed its own vernacular such as snaps, front and back yokes, fancy cuff and pocket treatments, and more. Mainstream designers picked up on Western for the first time during the Western music and dance fad of the late '70s, depicted in *Urban Cowboy*. Mainstream labels jumped on the Urban Cowboy mechanical bull and made Western design a fashion statement for the mass market. Very clearly, these designers derived

The real significance of the Urban Cowboy fad is that it brought Western wear to the general market for the first time.

their direction from traditional Western design but gave it a new spin with fabrics and styling twists that, in many cases, were over-the-top.

The opportunity for Western apparel companies to increase business was irresistible. However, the Urban Cowboy look was merely a costume for the mass market. It lacked the practical and cultural connections that had prompted the Western look in the first place. Suddenly, in 1979, Western was everywhere. But like all fickle fashion fads, it ended in 1981 as abruptly as it began.

The real significance of the Urban Cowboy fad is that Western reached the general market for the first time. Polo's Ralph Lauren, famous for identifying viable classic looks and giving them new life, worked his magic with Western. In a *Vanity Fair* interview (February, 1988) he made the dubious claim of having reinvented Western because, he said, on a trip to Denver he could not find a real Western shirt. His comments were just as patently wrong, obviously self-serving, and offensive to many in the Western apparel industry as Columbus's "discovery" of America was to the people already living here! But the truth would have made a less appealing story.

Upper left: Rockmount Ranch Wear, men's two-tone, rayon gabardine, 1940s. "The Missing Link": is it sportswear or is it Western? This is a good example of transitional Western design. It has the hallmarks of a new Western fashion with snaps, a back yoke, and stylized pockets but has not yet jelled into a completely distinct look. The long, contoured collar is typical of the 1940s.

Upper right: Prior, men's two-tone, 1940s. This transitional shirt is satin, a popular fabric with early rodeo cowboys. Its strong sportswear influences are its raglan style and sloping two-tone patch pockets. The shank buttons predate snaps.

Bottom left: Don Juan, California, men's gabardine embroidered shirt, 1950s. Mostly sportswear, it has a sport collar with loop, straight tails, single-button cuffs, buttonless pocket flaps with rope motif, genuine mother-of-pearl sew-through buttons, and early "S" sizing in the label. A Western influence is shown in the shirt's embroidery. Courtesy of Aardvark's Odd Ark, San Francisco, California.

Bottom right: Fleetline, men's shirt, 1950–60s. Its sportswear features are the scooped patch pockets (no flaps), sport collar, and simple cuffs with no sleeve plackets. Its Western features are front yokes, piping, and Dot diamond snaps with round inserts. Courtesy of Fine Clothing Daddy, Osaka, Japan.

In a May, 1988 **Tack 'n Togs** editorial, Dan DeWeese wrote:

A Designer Beef

Steve Weil, vice president at Rockmount Ranch Wear in Denver and third generation of the Rockmount Weils, came across an article in the February issue of **Vanity Fair** that raised his ire. The article, "Pardners in Style," was about how Ralph Lauren is single-handedly preserving the heritage of the Old West.

It seems the designer from the Bronx has gotten caught up in the romance of the West. Lauren bought himself a ranch in the Colorado Rockies and has outfitted it with a designer split-rail fence and designer log cabins for himself, his guests, and his ranch hands.

All that is interesting and even amusing to people involved in marketing Western apparel and riding equipment, but what got Weil's goat was an anecdote in the **Vanity Fair** article about how Lauren decided to make Western apparel. According to the article, Lauren was in Denver on business in 1977. "To his chagrin, he could not locate a single authentic, Western, snap-buttoned shirt anywhere," the article reads. "His fruitless search led to the creation of his Western Collection in 1978."

Now, Weil lives in Denver and Rockmount is based in Denver, as are several other Western apparel and equipment manufacturers. He shot off a response to the editor of **Vanity Fair** taking issue with the contention that Western shirts can't be found in Denver. Weil pointed out that his company is credited with originating snap shirt fasteners and that there are over thirty Western retailers listed in the phone book who have been in business since well before Mr. Lauren's unfortunate dilemma.

In short, either Ralph didn't look very hard, or he decided that the Western shirts in Denver were not "authentic" enough. Weil noted in his letter to the editor that, "There seems to be a pervasive arrogance on the East Coast that discounts the cultural contributions made by other regions."

Weil's point is well made. Such inaccurate and misleading information serves to illustrate that the Western industry needs to promote itself and Western culture.

Rockmount Ranch Wear was approached by a trendy men's jeans maker. The owners of the jeans company said that they "love Rockmount's story and signature designs." The two companies discussed Rockmount making a shirt line with a special joint label by both brands.

Rockmount, wary of being copied, was unwilling to send samples until an agreement was reached. After numerous conversations, their owners, managers, and designers came to Rockmount's showroom to review the entire line. This proved unlucky for Rockmount.

The showroom meeting went well, but the jeans company owners suddenly stopped returning phone calls and letters. Why the snag? Everyone had been so enthusiastic at the last meeting.

Rockmount learned a hard lesson a season later, when knockoffs hit the street fast and furious. The unlucky shirts were perfect copies of Rockmount's famous "sawtooth" pocket and saddle stitch designs.

The much more common method that unscrupulous companies pursue is to shop for new ideas. Some travel the high fashion markets of New York, Paris, and Milan. Others shop the vintage stores and from there provide a market survey from which designers select their new palette and direction.

Collectors need to be aware that knockoffs abound, their designs so scrupulously copied, an uncritical eye may not see the imitation for what it is.

—Steven E. Weil

For many in the industry, resentment faded as we realized that Ralph had done more for us than simply eat our lunch. What he did turned out to be a gift; he added tremendous value to the look. He raised the thirty-dollar retail-price ceiling the Western industry had imposed on itself. He opened up fabric selection. His nod to Americana gave it validity and brought it to a wider consumer market. Mainstream America—and the rest of the world—was introduced to a look, which, had it been in a traditional Western store, they would never have bought. He demonstrated very successfully that there was a market for high-end Western shirts. Western shirts were suddenly worth one hundred dollars! He gave credibility to classic Western design, and it became palatable to the upper end of the fashion market. These people began to accept Western as part of their lifestyle. They are a crossover market that continues to wear authentic Western brands.

And turn-about is fair play. By the 1990s many Western brands had adopted a "Tommy Hilfiger" look with bold stripes, color blocks, and single flapless pockets with an embroidered shield–type logo below. It clicked with the core Western market. Ironically, they went this direction to appeal to those being swayed by department store fashion but also ran the risk of alienating customers loyal to traditional Western looks. For years there was a Western customer who could buy the button-down look anywhere, not just at Western stores; the Urban Cowboy left a bad taste with some horse people and they adopted a non-Western, preppy look. If all the Western manufacturers had given up on traditional Western styling, it could have been its death. However, the look stayed alive and has again regained favor with most horse people.

Today Western shirts are prolific across the fashion spectrum. European jeanswear lines like Diesel, domestic brands like Fossil, and even hipster skateboard lines show Western shirts. Levi Strauss & Co. has returned to its Western roots, too. It seems like everybody is doing Western shirts. Every fashion line seems to be shopping for viable Western shirts to emulate. Whereas

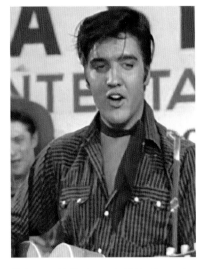

Elvis wore this Rockmount shirt in the movie Love Me Tender, 1957. Courtesy of Elvis Presley Enterprises, Inc.

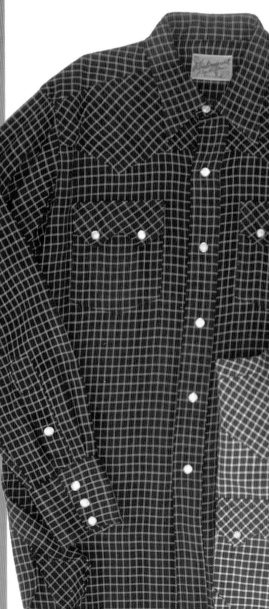

Ralph at least brought something new to the table, fashion lines now are simply copying existing Western shirts. Many designers are simply ripping off authentic Western brands.

Western Shirts Today

It used to be that a manufacturer could run a shirt design for years. These staple styles were the majority of the line, and only a small number of new designs were introduced each season. Those days are gone. Now, the proportion of staple styles to new introductions is reversed. The speed of fashion cycles has accelerated because of mass media. A trend no longer takes a couple of years to work itself across the country.

The Internet allowed the global economy to explode with instant, cheap communication. It is a different world since the Web was spun. Technology has changed everything. The Internet knocked down regional walls and replaced them with "global Windows." Rural life tapped into urban and global trends.

This global market has radically changed the manufacture and sale of Western shirts, just as it has changed everything else in the retail landscape. The arrival of big-box discounters has squeezed out the small mom-and-pop stores that were once the cornerstone of retail. There are an estimated 2,000 Western apparel stores in the United States today, just half of the number of Western retailers in business ten years ago. Price-driven retail undermines independent retailers and manufacturers alike. Low costs become paramount both in production and retail as big business strives for the lowest common denominator. It is bad for product diversity and for quality of life.

The American consumer has been conditioned to buy on sale, and rarely pays full price. The market is saturated with cheap imports and the entire apparel business is struggling. However, America's love for the vintage Western shirt grows, perhaps out of nostalgia for simpler, slower times.

Interestingly, there is a parallel today with the Great Depression. In the 1930s, people sought relief and happiness through their identity with the West, its heroes and its fashion. The recent trend of retro Western fashion from the golden age of Western wear is a tribute to good Western design and those who remain too stubborn to give it up. The resurgence of retro Western is perhaps a buoyant response to the turmoil of recession and 9/11.

But even if this is just another trend, it has reestablished Western design as an important part of classic American styling. Fashion trends come and go. Poor design goes into the scrap heap of history; good design transcends history. Good design does not embarrass you next year when you open your closet. It becomes your favorite shirt—now, next year, a decade from now. Your grandson or -daughter will love it years from now. Time is the ultimate test of good design, and classic Western shirts are holding their own.

Left: Rockmount Ranch Wear, men's windowpane plaids. Both fabrics are by Dan River. The shirt on the left is vintage, 1950s, the same model being worn by Elvis Presley, above. The shirt on the right is the remake from the late 1990s. The construction, collar size, and fabric of the two are identical; only the labels and snaps differ: the vintage shirt has genuine mother-of-pearl snaps and the label says, "original model;" the remake label says "Made in U.S.A."

CHAPTER 2

★ ★

VINTAGE SHIRTS AS
COLLECTIBLES

Collecting vintage Western shirts had its roots in the early 1980s but took several years to gel into a movement. Vintage shirts were relegated to thrift store status until the early 1990s. A Japanese fad for vintage Americana, including jeans and Western shirts, took hold in the late 1980s. This solidified a grass roots industry where pickers from home and abroad traveled the country buying choice pieces from thrift and vintage stores. Large rag wholesalers sorted bales of used clothing to find the higher-value pearls. Today, good vintage is found in museums, vintage stores, and on the Internet—rarely, if ever, in thrift stores. Less-collectible generic designs and brands are still cheap and plentiful.

Collectors seek the higher-value pieces because of their unique design, fine fabric, and quality construction. Shopping vintage stores gives a quick picture of the range—in age and design—of shirts on the market. The rare shirts are expensive and showcased. Prices indicate rarity, demand, and intrinsic quality. Brands known for quality and creative designs are more collectible. Also, shirts from the 1960s and earlier tend to be priced higher than those made later.

Plain shirts, typically imported since the 1970s, were a commodity product when they were made, and their prices today reflect the lower quality. Generic designs, low-end fabrics, and imports are plentiful and cheap in thrift stores. Shirts that make a statement cost more to make and reflect that value now. The better shirts and collectible brands represent an era of higher standards; they were constructed with quality and care because the people who made them had respect for and knew the needs of the people who wore them. No one could conceive that their value would rise over time.

Most Vintage Shirts are Men's

Men's shirts represent the bulk of the total Western shirt production. Women and children's shirts amount to less than 20 percent of total production. This is because traditionally, Western wear appeals most strongly to men. One collector and vintage retailer, Taras Prodanink (Play Clothes, Studio City, California) says that the availability of product for women is a problem because "there is a sizing issue: people were smaller." If a collector wants to find a women's garment to wear, finding larger-size pieces is difficult because fewer were made in the first place.

Below: Unmarked, men's gabardine embroidered shirt, 1940s. A smoker's dream with burning cigarette chenille embroidery on front, back, and cuffs. Also features steer-head embroidery, smile pockets with sew-on tabs, enamel snaps, and piping. Courtesy of Cowgirls of the West Museum, Cheyenne, Wyoming.

No Pricing Standard

There is no consistent standard for pricing vintage clothing. Factors such as demand, condition, and rarity, as well as original packaging, affect the price. "New/old" is a rarified category highly sought after by collectors. This is the "dead stock" that has escaped the ravages of time. Sometimes it is found in wholesale quantities—forgotten in storage—or it surfaces as a single piece that was put away new and never worn. Although the Web has created a global marketplace, pricing remains variable. Generally, pricing seems to fall into four ranges:

$300+: extremely fine, rare, ornate shirts

$100–$300: highly ornate embroideries, pre-1960

$25–$100: nicely detailed basic makes in good vintage fabrics, pre-1970

Less than $25: generic, mass-produced commodity styles, including imports, since 1970s

Of course, pricing changes along with trends, so these figures have a limited window of accuracy.

The original cost of the garment is in direct proportion to the volume produced. Tailor-made shirts by Rodeo Ben and Nudie were very expensive and out of the reach of the public when new. These early designs were "one-off" custom makes for celebrities like Roy Rogers and Gene Autry. Later they went to limited production runs but remained much more expensive than production-made garments. By the same logic, the more expensive the ready-to-wear garment, the lower the volume it was produced in. It is not uncommon to find only a single surviving example of the best highly stylized designs.

The challenge faced by early shirt manufacturers was to factory-produce fine, special treatments similar to those of the tailors. The good, commercially made shirts were never mass produced. These shirts have finely crafted details that were possible only with the workmanship of skilled shirt makers. The shirts were labor intensive and not suited to high automation. The quality of that time's top factory-made goods is similar to what is custom-made quality today. This was possible because the good designers innovated production techniques and treatments that were practical for factory production. This was an era when fabric was the biggest cost factor, followed by labor.

Western shirt design became simpler over the years for a number of reasons. As the discount chains began carrying Western wear, they demanded cheaper products. Many manufacturers catered to these stores, so their entire production changed over time. Also, domestic United States labor costs began rising in the 1950s, giving rise to the middle class. By the 1970s, labor costs had eclipsed fabric costs, fundamentally changing the economics of apparel costs. The market had set perceived values for Western shirts, making it very difficult to produce and sell the highly stylized designs at prices customers were willing to pay.

Special treatments gave way to efficient factory automation of most brands. Cheaper labor costs in third-world countries brought about the decline of the entire U.S. textile industry.

Above: Miller Western Wear, men's rayon gabardine navy/turquoise two-tone, 1940s. Boldly colored, this shirt features smile pockets with embroidered arrows, piping, five-snap shotgun cuffs, a slim-fit size stamp on the tail that predates tag sizes, and a surged tail. Courtesy of Santa Monica Vintage, Tokyo, Japan.

The Western industry had a self-imposed retail price ceiling on shirts of about thirty dollars, above which there was little volume. It took mainstream fashion designers such as Ralph Lauren to kick-start the high-end market back to life after years of simpler and cheaper makes, mostly made of cotton/polyester blends. Retro Western-shirt designs in fine fabrics enjoyed a comeback when designer lines copied earlier works of the Western shirt companies and introduced them to the mainstream in the early 1980s. There were two positive consequences of this: the thirty-dollar glass ceiling was broken and Western design was validated by mainstream fashion worldwide.

One of the interesting questions central to vintage shirts is, "Why do people collect them?" Steven E. Weil interviews some collectors to find out.

Interview with *Ronny Weiser* ★★★★★★★★★★★★★★★★★★★★

Ronny Weiser contacted me in the early 1990s when he was researching Rockmount for a rockabilly newsletter he publishes. I met him later at a trade show. "Rockin' Ronny" was wearing a pink Nudie suit. We later went to his house, virtually a Western museum filled with vintage clothing and memorabilia. I don't think I have ever met anyone else with a collection of Rockmount larger than mine.

Q: What motivates you to collect vintage Western shirts?

A: When I got my first pair of blue jeans in 1957, I didn't call it "collecting," but instead, "living the American dream and enjoying the spirit of the West."

Q: When did you start collecting?

A: About five years ago, with eBay, my collecting became more active, but originally I began in 1957.

Q: How many pieces are in your collection?

A: I don't know, maybe 1,000 or more.

Q: What is the least you have paid for an item?

A: Twenty-five cents.

Q: The most?

A: One hundred and sixty dollars.

Q: What period do you collect?

A: Mostly 1950s, but also some 1940s, and even more modern periods if the items have a classic 1950s look.

Q: What brands do you collect?

A: For shirts, mainly Rockmount, Tem-Tex, Miller, Levi, H Bar C, Karman, Cowboy Joe, and Panhandle Slim.

Q: What styles do you collect?

A: 1950s Western wear, hepcat threads, and rockabilly rebel—style duds.

Q: Anything you would like to add?

A: I don't really consider myself a "collector," but instead I think of myself as a fan and enthusiastic supporter of the American way of life, from rockabilly music to 1950s Cadillacs, from classic Western wear to Tex Avery cartoons! And much, much more, of course!

Interview with *Kim Naddeo*

Kim Naddeo is a musician from Texas who collects vintage Western shirts. He contacted me to find out more about his Rockmount shirts.

Q: What motivates you to collect and when did you start?

A: I'm a musician, and my band was getting ready to start a summer tour. I went into some stores in the West End of Dallas to shop for stage clothes. I found a new/old stock Rockmount shirt in a Western store and loved it from the moment I tried it on. Unfortunately, it was the store's last one. I couldn't find any more in Dallas before I started the tour, so I just had the one. But the shirt made quite an impression and turned heads; people knew we were musicians before we had even played a note. I think that's important since they come to see a show. Plus, I not only looked like a "rock star," but it made me feel like one too. The lightweight material and fit is not only beneficial to cowboys, it works great for musicians in the sweltering Texas hill country summer heat, playing guitar, and moving gear! As soon as I returned, I had to find more.

I contacted Rockmount and started to look for vintage shirts on eBay. In the process of seeking out my personal style preferences, I began to learn more about vintage Rockmount and H Bar C. I also started to recognize historical elements and the types of vintage shirts that were in movies I'd been watching all along. This was the birth of my deep appreciation of vintage Western shirts.

Q: How many pieces are in your collection?

A: Haven't counted, but I am on my way to becoming the Imelda Marcos of vintage Western shirts.

Q: What is the least you have paid? The most?

A: I've paid between ten and thirty dollars, but have bid much more on eBay and lost.

Q: What period do you collect?

A: Anything that tickles my fancy. Maybe I'll zero in on particular years after I learn more.

Q: What brands do you collect?

A: Rockmount mainly and some H Bar C.

Q: What styles do you collect?

A: My favorite is the Rockmount Quarter Horse pockets and saddle stitching. A bit of flash, yet understated and very stylish.

Interview with *Ron Rico* ✳✳✳✳✳✳✳✳✳✳✳✳✳✳✳✳✳✳✳✳✳✳

Ron Rico is a Canadian collector I corresponded with after we bid against each other for a vintage Rockmount shirt.

Q: What motivates you to collect?

A: I wear the clothing I collect because affordable fashion today is either conservative—as in men's dress shoes being either black or brown, or it is trashy—as in MTV. Also, unlike vintage Western shirts, most of today's clothing that I like is priced way beyond my reach. And finally, the quality of clothing being made today is inferior to what was just standard quality a few decades ago.

Q: When did you start collecting?

A: I started in 1999.

Q: How many pieces in your collection?

A: Including boots, shoes, shirts, ties, pants, jacket, and suits: approximately 150.

Q: What is the most you have paid for a shirt?

A: I paid sixty-seven dollars and fifty cents for a dead stock 1950s Rockmount Ranch Wear shirt.

Q: What period do you collect?

A: I collect 1930s, '40s, '50s, and '60s, with my target decades being 1940s to the '50s.

Q: What shirt brands do you collect?

A: Among others, Tem-Tex, Panhandle Slim, Prior, Rockmount Ranch Wear, Trego's Lasso, Niver, and Canadian brands like Sprung, Caravan, and Riley and McCormick.

Q: *What styles do you collect?*

A: *I like rayon or rayon gab Western shirts from the 1950s. Because I wear the vintage I collect, I stay away from the heavily embroidered H Bar C shirts as I don't want to have people think I'm nuts (I live in Vancouver where nobody, and I mean nobody, walks around wearing any Western at all).*

Q: *Anything you would like to add?*

A: *You shouldn't have asked! The best thing about vintage Western is that it is affordable for almost any price range. A top-of-the-line, dead stock 1950s Western rayon shirt from a quality maker such as Karman will cost usually no more than one hundred dollars and often a lot less. Compared with a shirt by a contemporary designer like Liz Claiborne or Calvin Klein, it's an incredible value. Most high-quality, vintage Western shirts can be purchased for less than fifty dollars. When one compares workmanship, quality of materials, and the impeccable design of so many of the items, the value is even more outstanding.*

Cost aside, the biggest surprise for me as a relatively new collector is the adventurous nature of the designers working at the time. The artistic freedom enjoyed by the designers of the 1940s and '50s is quite fantastic. Shirts had scores of unique features like topstitching and embroideries, two-tones, and insets. The '50s saw men's clothing being designed in pink and black, which is hard to imagine the average man of today wearing.

Some of the best examples of this artistic license can be found in Rockmount Ranch Wear's Western shirts from the 1940s and '50s. The elaborate yokes, stitching, tricky cuffs, intricate pocket details, and excellent array of fabrics are amazing and make much of the Western wear produced today look anemic.

The real testament to the quality of this clothing is that there is still so much of it around after fifty or sixty years! How much of what was produced in the 1990s will be with us sixty years from now? I have had in my possession, at one time or another, clothing from some of the world's top designers—Prada, Versace, Brioni, Hermes, Gucci, etc. I've had the opportunity to closely examine shirts and slacks that retailed for $600 or $700 and up. And while some of this clothing is very beautiful and extremely well made, most of the items produced for the average man and woman of the 1940s and '50s are equal to this quality and often exceeded it.

Interview with *Robert Rubin* ★

Robert Rubin is a collector from California. He had a very rare 1940s Rockmount gabardine shirt with steer head embroidery. It is the only one I have ever seen like it. It was too small for him so he traded it to me for a new shirt so the original could be in our archives. We have reintroduced it in the Rockmount line.

Q: What do you collect?

A: *I have a passion for collecting classic '50s, '60s, and '70s Americana. My entire house is decorated in this theme.*

Q: When did you start collecting?

A: *Ten years ago.*

Q: How many shirts are in your collection?

A: *My collection is at about one hundred shirts. Some I buy and then sell and others I will keep forever.*

Q: What is the least you have paid for one?

A: *Two dollars.*

Q: The most?

A: *One hundred dollars.*

Q: What brands do you collect?

A: *Brands I have are H Bar C, Dee Cee Western, Rockmount, Levi Strauss & Co., and Mustang.*

Q: What styles do you collect?

A: *I collect all styles from simple daily-wear Western shirts, to a few that I'm scared to wear out!*

Q: Anything you would like to add?

A: *I like shirts that are different; stuff that you don't see everyday. I think there are many collectors out there who feel the same way and wouldn't mind paying some extra bucks for a shirt like that.*

Rockmount Ranch Wear men's two-tone gabardine with steer embroidery, 1946. This rare, early shirt is one of Rockmount's first, made at a shirt plant in Emmaus, Pennsylvania.

The classic '40s design has hand-maneuvered chain-stitch chenille embroidery, smile pockets, and piping. Design features include single-point cuffs, early enamel snaps that predate pearl snaps, and tail gussets. Single-point cuffs without a sleeve placket were a later alteration. Note the back pleats are a sportswear element and give a tapered, slimming look. Courtesy of Rockmount, Denver, Colorado.

CHAPTER 3
★ ★ ★

DESIGN ELEMENTS
OF WESTERN SHIRTS

The beauty of Western fashion is its diversity of design, a reflection of the rugged individuals personified by the American cowboy. Even those who wear Western shirts now define themselves as individuals and nonconformists. Western shirts made from 1930 to 1980 encompass an incredible range of styles. However, beginning in the 1970s the diversity declined due to the stifling nature of mass production and cheap imports. At that point, keeping the price low prevailed over keeping quality high. The economics of labor costs in the United States had changed. Manufacturers reduced the special treatments in an effort to hold rising labor costs. Ironically, some modern trends have been towards a generic and uniform Western shirt, the antithesis of what made Western wear popular in the first place.

Over the years, Western shirt design has developed its own vernacular based on its myriad elements. Early shirts were intended to be a departure from conventional fashion. The whole point was to make a distinctive shirt nothing like what was conventional and available. Better commercially made shirts through the 1950s and into the 1960s were in many ways like fine custom-made shirts. They were highly stylized, with complex special treatments and details, and their designs range in every way imaginable.

The origin of distinctive design elements in Western shirts is interesting and instructive. Early fabric choices were restricted by the Depression, and later, World War II. Some of the earliest Western shirt fabrics were heavy, made of suiting no one had ever thought of using in shirts before, such as worsted wool, wool gabardine, and textured rayons. Later, increased demand allowed companies to make their own fabrics specifically for Western shirts.

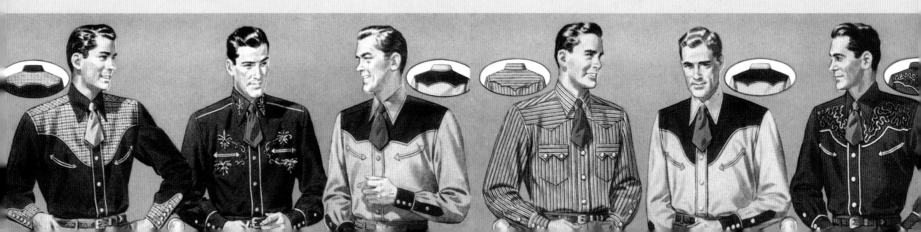

Design elements for Western shirts are many and varied—part of what makes them so interesting to collect. Flap pockets, piping, and cavalry bibs reflect a military influence. Jack Weil recalls adapting a U.S. Navy five-point-star embroidery machine to create a single-point arrow to finish a pocket. Here is a list of design elements that characterize Western shirts to watch for in your collecting.

Fit

Originally, the fit of Western shirts was a total departure from conventional men's shirts, which were boxy and featured Victorian-era removable collars until the 1920s. Western shirts were "form-fit" and flattering to the slim physique. From the practical standpoint of someone who would use them as active wear, the less loose they were, the less likely they were to snag. The fit was an important selling point for Western shirts; it characterized the entire shirt. Neck and sleeve sizing was exclusively the standard for more than fifty years. Fitted shirts were made in more than twenty sizes including neck size and sleeve lengths. This type of sizing is still made today but has largely been replaced by Small-Medium-Large sizing. Relaxed-fit followed with the same S-M-L designation. The S-M-L sizing enabled manufacturers to streamline production and reduce inventory at wholesale and retail levels. It also helped with exports as the previous inch-based sizing measurement is not used by most countries.

Women's shirts, on the other hand, were conventionally form-fit, and women's Western shirts followed this tradition. While women's shirts were sized for women, they tended to be driven by men's Western styles, often matching men's designs and fabrics. In fact, matching "his 'n' hers" shirts became an important selling point for decades. Traditionally, sales of women's Western shirts are substantially lower than men's. Since the Urban Cowboy fad, mainstream fashion has had a big impact on women's Western shirts. Western designers began adopting mainstream fashion elements, and fashion designers pick up Western elements from time to time.

Fashion is cyclical and so is fit. While men's shirts were loose fitting until the advent of Western wear, slim-fitting neck and sleeve sizing was standard until relaxed fit came into vogue in the late 1980s. Now there is a high-fashion revival of slim-fit for young men and women. When Western fashion came into being it was mainly popular with young, slim men. As the consumer for Western wear aged, looser fits became popular as it forgives and hides heavier builds. Now slim-fit retro-Western is appealing to young men again. The fashion cycle has come around full circle.

Left: Miller Stockman Supply Company. Courtesy of Jack A. Weil, Denver, Colorado.

FINE FABRICS
STYLED THE WAY YOU WANT THEM
From the top manufacturers
The Wrangler has selected the most-wanted shirts
For style-conscious Westerners

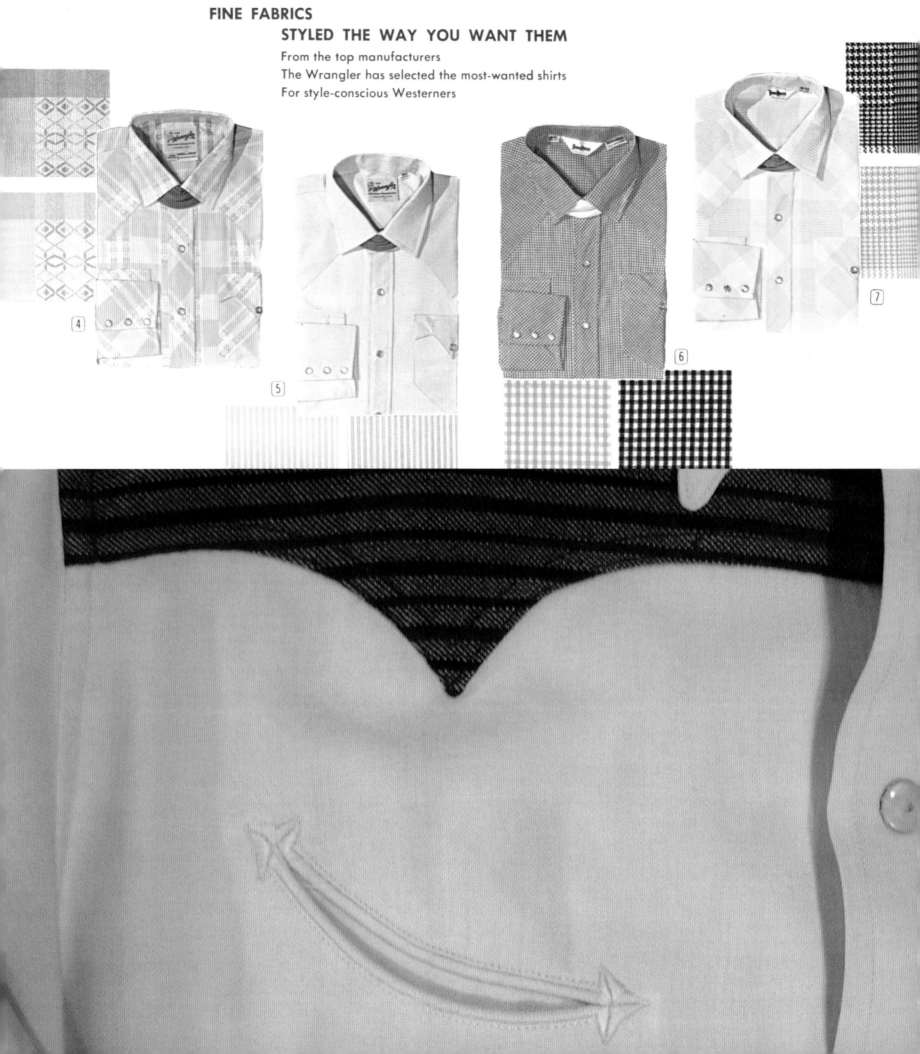

Fabric

The beauty of Western shirts has much to do with fabric. It is helpful to categorize shirts by fabric. The earliest shirts were custom or homemade. There were no shirts out in the general market yet. Cowboys, performers, and actors had to make their own garments or have them made. They desired a costume to differentiate themselves from spectators and other performers. Fabric was key, but choices were limited.

Tailor-made shirts often used suiting such as heavy worsted wool, gabardine, and rayon. One of the reasons tailors used this fabric in shirts is that they already had it for the suits they made before they got into the shirt business. During the 1920s and '30s, these heavy fabrics were mostly solids and stripes. It only takes a few yards to make a shirt, so their demand was too low to have the fabric produced by the textile mills. Since these suiting fabrics had not been used previously in shirts, it was a fresh and distinct look, but the shirts were heavy and impractical, hot to wear, and could not be washed.

Once Western shirts went into commercial production in the 1930s, a much bigger selection of fabric became available because the mills could produce specifically for the Western market. Rodeo cowboys liked flashy satins (which have now been in use for decades, since the 1930s). The early factory-made shirts were mostly solid fabrics in simple makes with flap pockets, shank buttons, and no front yoke. The fabric was commonly cotton sateen and wool gabardine. Many companies made this style, including Pendleton, Levi, and Miller. It was popular and continued later with more flourish in the 1940s by companies including Rockmount, Prior, and H Bar C. This make was an early-Western lifestyle statement, not a costume like the embroidered and more ornate, flamboyant styles of the celebrities.

Back in the 1930s fabric was only twenty-eight to thirty-six inches wide, and so required at least three yards per shirt. Looms got wider over the years—forty-five inches, and now sixty inches. Fabric widened as technology improved, resulting in more efficient yields.

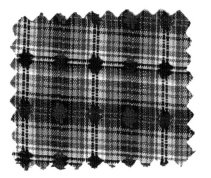

Above: Miller & Co. J. M. McDonald wholesale line sheet, 1957. Courtesy of Miller International, Denver, Colorado.

Left, above: The Wrangler of Cheyenne catalog, 1963. Courtesy of Miller International, Denver, Colorado.

Left, below: Vaquero Fashions, Taylor-Berke in California, men's wool suiting gabardine two-tone, 1940s. Features enamel snaps and smile pockets with embroidered arrows. Heavy suiting was used in early Western shirts because designers wanted to differentiate them from conventional fashion and had little else to choose from that was not otherwise used in conventional shirting. Courtesy of Ronny Weiser, Las Vegas, Nevada.

Right: Miller & Co. wholesale line sheet, 1961–63. Courtesy of Miller International, Denver, Colorado.

LOT NO. 911-28   SELL: $5.95

* John Wolfe Luminous All Cotton Floral Broadcloth with Colored Grounds, Washfast, No Iron Finish.
* Form-Fit "High Rise" Yoke Model.
* Two-Point "Lazy U" Back Yoke, "Panel Back".
* "Teton" Pockets, One Snap Each Flap.
* Permanent Collar Stays.
* Fitted Cuffs with Three Snaps.
* Nickel Rim "Tec" Pearl Snaps.

COLORS: BLUE FLAME, TORCH RED, AMBER
PACK: 2/12 SIZE, COLOR AND SLEEVE LENGTH
SIZES: 14 to 16½
August Delivery

Later, as Western design became more stylized, and the makes differentiated enough from conventional styling to achieve the goal of a distinct Western look, conventional fabrics were used, greatly expanding their market. The commercially made shirts tended to be made with more practical, lighter-weight fabrics because the volume desired was large enough to enable the mills to produce them.

The new fabrics ran the gamut; all colors of cotton, rayon, and acetate and constructions of solids, plaids, stripes, dobbies, and prints. Many of the brands used a very wide range of fabrics over the years. The primary limitation tended to be a cost issue. The target price of the shirt dictated the amount spent on fabric. Fabric costs were the higher proportion of the total cost of making shirts until U.S. labor costs began rising in the 1960s, changing the economics of production permanently. Fabric costs were the main variable cost of a shirt, especially in the early years.

Many shirts can be dated by their fabrics:

Wool gabardine and other wool weaves: 1930s to the '50s, reintroduced in the 1990s.

Rayon gabardine: 1940s to the '50s, reintroduced in the late 1980s.

Acetates, nylons: 1940s to the '60s, thereafter replaced by polyester. (Nylon/cotton blends reduced shrinkage but were not practical because they melted when ironed.)

Woven satin: 1930s to the present.

Knitted satin: Since the 1970s.

All-cotton: 1930s to the '60s, in various weaves including sateen, solid sheeting, plaids, checks, and prints. All-cotton gave way to no-iron blends in the 1960s but has been popular again since the 1980s.

Polyester and poly/cotton blends: 1960s to the present.

Right: Vaquero Fashion, men's suit with chenille embroidery, 1940s. Features heavy wool gabardine suiting, a very long collar, smile pockets, shotgun cuffs, and red pipings. Courtesy of La Rosa Vintage Boutique, San Francisco, California.

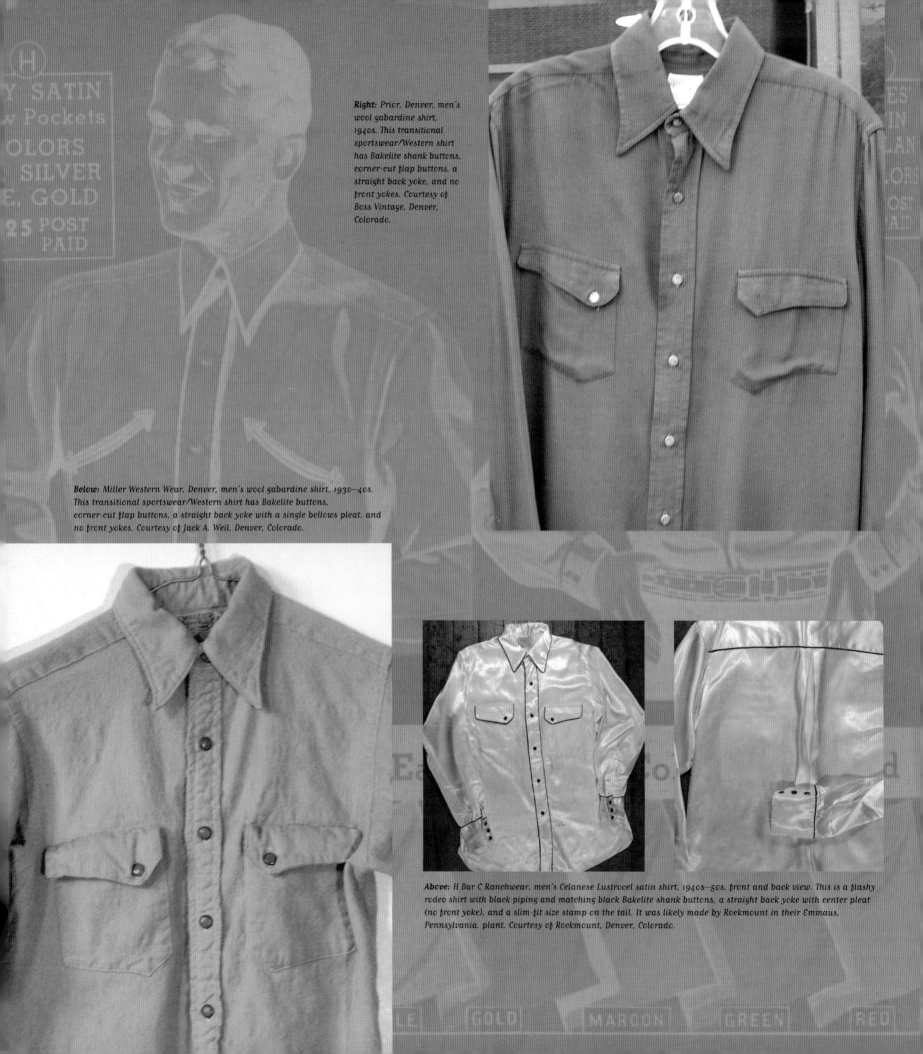

Right: *Prior, Denver, men's wool gabardine shirt, 1940s. This transitional sportswear/Western shirt has Bakelite shank buttons, corner-cut flap buttons, a straight back yoke, and no front yokes. Courtesy of Boss Vintage, Denver, Colorado.*

Below: *Miller Western Wear, Denver, men's wool gabardine shirt, 1930–40s. This transitional sportswear/Western shirt has Bakelite buttons, corner-cut flap buttons, a straight back yoke with a single bellows pleat, and no front yokes. Courtesy of Jack A. Weil, Denver, Colorado.*

Above: *H Bar C Ranchwear, men's Celanese Lustrocel satin shirt, 1940s–50s, front and back view. This is a flashy rodeo shirt with black piping and matching black Bakelite shank buttons, a straight back yoke with center pleat (no front yoke), and a slim-fit size stamp on the tail. It was likely made by Rockmount in their Emmaus, Pennsylvania, plant. Courtesy of Rockmount, Denver, Colorado.*

Above: Levi Strauss & Co., men's satin shirt, 1930s–40s. This early transitional shirt has the "rodeo" label, a flashy fabric likely intended for cowboys who wanted to differentiate themselves from dudes in town on a Saturday night or during rodeos. It features sew-through buttons, corner-cut pockets, tail gussets, winged triple-button cuffs, and no front yokes. Courtesy of Ronny Weiser, Las Vegas, Nevada.

Above 101, men's wool gabardine shirt, 1930s–40s. This is a defunct brand named for the famous Oklahoma cattle ranch/Wild West show where Tom Mix got his start. This transitional sportswear/Western shirt is lined and has Bakelite shank buttons, corner-cut flap buttons, a straight back yoke with a single bellows pleat, tail gussets, and no front yokes. Courtesy of Traditions West, Cody, Wyoming.

Above: H Bar C Ranchwear, men's wool gabardine shirt, 1940s, front and back view. This transitional sportswear/Western shirt is lined, has Bakelite shank buttons, corner-cut flap buttons, a straight back yoke with a single bellows pleat, and no front yokes. Courtesy of Cody Antique Mall, Cody, Wyoming.

Yokes

The word *yoke* is a Western term, derived from the wooden harness worn by oxen to pull wagons. Yoke fabrics are usually a little heavier—made with an extra ply—and sewn from the shoulder seam down over the body of the shirt, front and back. In conventional shirt design, shirts can have straight yokes across the back but seldom in front. The Western yoke is always stylized; sometimes it is pointed, less frequently, it is contoured. All shirts of woven fabrics have a back yoke; most pre-1990s Western shirts have a front yoke too.

What do yokes do? They serve as a primary design element, but they may have had practical value too. From a design standpoint, shirt yokes accentuate broad shoulders. They also let cowboys look and feel different from everyone else. From a practical standpoint, yokes might have been an adaptation of the cowboy habit of wearing scarves as another fabric layer to protect them from the elements. It has been said that some cowboys actually had scarves sewn down on their shirts to help shed water and provide a layer of insulation against the sun or the cold.

While yokes are considered a key element in Western design, the early Western shirts of the 1920s and '30s often had none in the front. Their straight back yokes gave rise to fancy curved and pointed versions. Fancier yokes emerged in the late 1930s but did not come in much variety until the 1940s. Highly stylized yokes came into vogue by the early 1950s. Piping, which came into use in the 1930s, accentuated them.

Yokes come in a limitless number of shapes. Some are curved and scalloped, others are straight and simple. Most front yokes are single-point: V-shaped. Most back yokes are curved, although some are single-point, even triple-point.

Many highly embroidered shirts have no front yokes, so there is room for more coverage on the front. Front yokes are also rare on bib-front shirts. Yokes work especially well in two-tone designs that contrast. Yokes are also effective in directional patterns, such as plaids and stripes: the yoke runs one way and the body the other.

Left: Ranch-Man Western Wear, Denver, men's cotton, plaid dobby shirt, 1950–60s. Features a highly stylized "fishtail," a scalloped-motif front yoke, contoured pocket flaps, a sleeve placket with decorative embroidered edge, and Rau white marbled snaps. It is interesting that this design has expensive special treatments but its pockets are on the bias, a cheaper alternative to matched, which is considered better construction. Courtesy of Ronny Weiser, Las Vegas, Nevada.

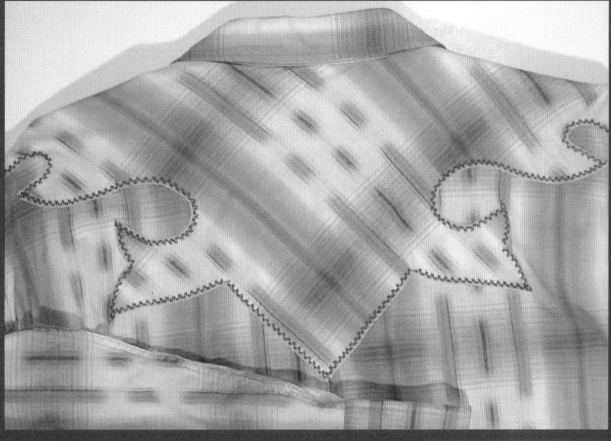

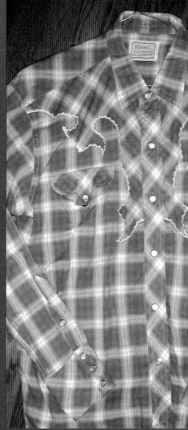

Above: Ranch-Man Western Wear, Denver, men's cotton plaid dobby shirt, 1950—60s. The "fish-tail" yoke required a lot of skill to set. Courtesy of Ronny Weiser, Las Vegas, Nevada.

Right, above: H Bar C, men's shadow plaid, 1960s. Has a highly stylized Texas state motif on front yokes and pockets. Features a decorative embroidered edge and round snaps. Everything about this make required extra skill and work, and so was more expensive. Courtesy of Richard Doherty, Dallas, Texas.

Right: Rockmount Ranch Wear, men's plaid dobby shirt, 1950s. Has a highly stylized double-pointed yoke with arch-like Gothic window, triple-point "batwing" pocket flaps, inside-hanging pockets, and smoke hex snaps. All these special details added cost to the garment. Courtesy of Rockmount, Denver, Colorado.

Far right: Karman, men's cotton print, 1960s. Has a highly contoured hook motif with decorative embroidered edge, a single-snap cuff, and no placket snap. Courtesy of Boss Vintage, Denver, Colorado.

Below: Tanbark, a defunct label, men's herringbone shirt, 1940s—50s. An early version of what became a major trend forty years later, it features mitered front and back yokes, a lining, neck and sleeve size stamps predating size tags, vertical triple snaps, mother-of-pearl snaps, and five-snap contoured shotgun cuffs. Courtesy of Candy's Vintage, Boulder, Colorado.

Below, middle: Goatroper by PMC, men's two-tone cotton blend cape shirt, 1970s—80s. A defunct, but interesting name, this contoured design came out in the last revival of this style. Courtesy of Hex Hive Vintage, Nara, Japan.

Below, right: H Bar C Ranchwear, men's windowpane cotton cape shirt, 1960s. This triple-snap version is an early design predating the major trend ten years later. Courtesy of Boss Vintage, Denver, Colorado.

There are countless yoke styles in Western design. Here are some of the major yoke styles:

Two-toned scalloped was strong in the 1940s and '50s and continues to be made today. This is a classic Western design especially associated with early cowboy actors and musicians through modern days.

Yokes go wild and crazy in the 1950s. You can find them in almost any shape, as can be seen in Rockmount's saddle-stitched pink plaid. The back yoke forms a highly stylized, deep double-point. They also did a triple-point back yoke.

Continuous yoke/pocket flap treatments show up in the 1950s and were made in countless variations. Panhandle Slim made a diamond-shaped cutout. Tem-Tex did a wonderful "moustache"

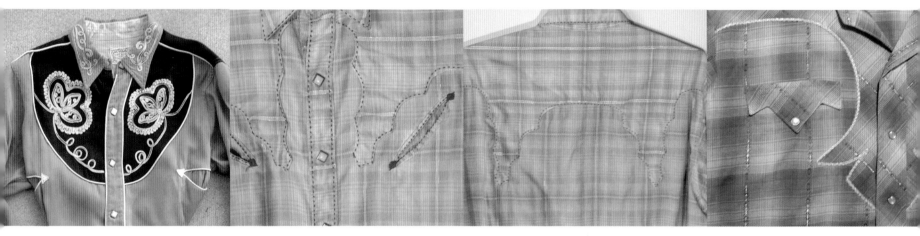

Above: Las Vegas by Country Joe, men's two-tone embroidered shirt, 1950s. This shirt features lined gabardine with soutache bonnaz embroidery, smile pockets with sew-on tabs, and diamond snaps. Courtesy of Cookie Michael, Romancing the Range, Houston, Texas.

Above: Rockmount Ranch Wear, men's cotton plaid with gold lurex, 1950s, front and back view. These scalloped front yokes go to an extreme. The shirt features a saddle-stitch accent, smile pockets with arrow embroidery, and gold-rimmed diamond snaps that coordinate with the lurex stripe. Courtesy of Rockmount, Denver, Colorado.

Above: Wolfe's Sportsmen's Headquarters, Salt Lake City, men's plaid dobby with silver lurex stripe, 1960s. Features large-radius contour yokes with a decorative embroidered edge, triple-point "batwing" pocket flaps with inside-hanging pockets, and round snaps. Courtesy of Ronny Weiser, Las Vegas, Nevada.

Below: Panhandle Slim, men's shirt, 1950s. Features a one-piece yoke/diamond-cutout pocket flap on patch pocket, and black snaps. Courtesy of Ronny Weiser, Las Vegas, Nevada.

Below: Tem-Tex Sportswear, men's plaid, 1950–60s. Features a tapadero motif with bonnaz decorative trim, inside-hanging pockets, and a slim-size collar band stamp. Courtesy of Ronny Weiser, Las Vegas, Nevada.

Below: Rockmount Ranch Wear, men's eyelash plaid, 1950s. Features a one-piece yoke/pocket-flap treatment. Courtesy of Rockmount, Denver, Colorado.

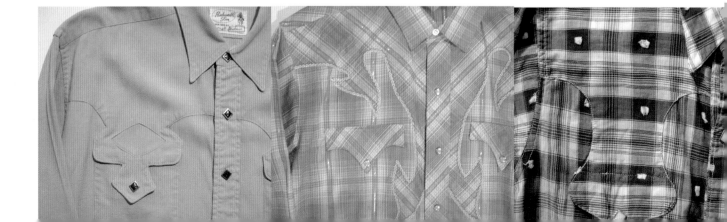

Below: This border print from the 1960s, likely by Prior, has smile pockets.

back yoke. (See front yokes of this shirt under section on pockets, page 56.) Rockmount made hundreds of fabrics in its contoured "stirrup" style.

Highly stylized shapes with a decorative embroidery outline were popular in the 1950s and '60s. They were contoured in all sorts of shapes and fabrics. Karman did a plaid "spade" treatment. Ranch-Man did a plaid "fishtail" treatment front and back (see pages 42 and 43). Tem-Tex did a plaid shirt with a long "Tapadero" motif on the front

Cape yokes, first seen in the 1940s or '50s, had a long run. Tanbark, a defunct Western label, did a mitered stripe with three vertical snaps. H Bar C did a triple-snap version in the 1960s. Goatroper, a small label but interesting brand, made this contoured version when cape shirts had a revival in the 1970s and '80s.

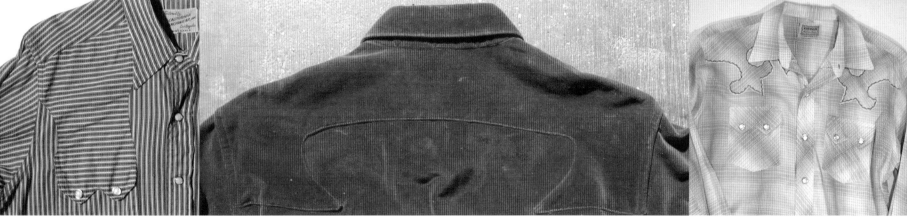

Printed yokes first showed up in the 1950s. Rockmount's engineered border print has the effect of front and back yokes without separate fabric plies. This early example led to a huge trend in the 1980s with Western and Indian prints.

Below: Rockmount Ranch Wear, men's border print, 1950s, back and front view. This early engineered print predates a major trend twenty years later. The shirt features single-point cuffs, hex snaps, and inside-hanging pockets, a more costly design done so the pocket does not interfere with the fabric pattern. Courtesy of Rockmount, Denver, Colorado.

Above, left: California Ranchwear, Los Angeles, men's rayon stripe shirt, 1940–50s. This shirt features a one-piece tapered yoke/"sawtooth" pocket-flap treatment, a long contoured collar, and round snaps. Courtesy of Ronny Weiser, Las Vegas, Nevada.

Above, middle: Panhandle Slim/Lou Taubert Ranch Outfitters, private label, 1950s. Features a velvet hatchet-shaped, cut-out back yoke. Courtesy of Cody Antique Mall, Cody, Wyoming.

Above: Karman, men's cotton/silver lurex plaid, 1960s. Features a spade-front yoke with decorative embroidered edging and round snaps. The special yoke treatment is costly, but the biased pockets are a cheaper alternative to matching the pattern to the body. Courtesy of Ronny Weiser, Las Vegas, Nevada.

Jack A. Weil had the idea to make snap shirts before World War II precluded the use of brass in consumer goods. He went to the Scovill plant in Waterbury, Connecticut, to develop snaps for shirts and manufacturing equipment to attach them. Scovill declined at first, saying it was a "misapplication." Jack, persevering and determined, scolded Scovill, "Dammit, if I bought and paid for them and ate them as Post Toasties it's none of your business!" Senior management agreed and together they developed the first shirt snaps and the machinery to attach them.

Clockwise, starting below: *Miller Western Wear, men's shirt folded in a box, 1930s. The "holy grail" of the earliest Miller shirts, it features piping, tabs on smile pockets, sew-through buttons that predate snaps, and three-button cuffs. Courtesy of Miller International, Denver, Colorado.*

Glover Guaranteed Quality, men's wool pullover, 1920–30s. Features a lined collar, a box-pleated front placket, sew-through buttons, a single-corner patch pocket, and a tail gusset. Courtesy of David Little, Cody Antique Mall, Cody, Wyoming.

Bond Bros. Pendleton, Oregon, men's polished cotton with button-down collar, 1900–20s. A rare, very early shirt. Features large sew-through buttons, plain flap pockets, a double-button sleeve placket, a single-button cuff, and a deep tail contour with gusset. Courtesy of Cowboy Land & Cattle, Cody, Wyoming.

Miller Western Wear, men's rayon gabardine shirt, 1930–40s. Features sew-through buttons predating shank buttons, piping, smile pockets with tabs, and tail gussets. The size stamp on the tail predates size tags. Courtesy of Susan Adams, Richmond, Virginia.

Jack A. Weil developed the "duo-stud" (see below) in the late 1940s to solve the problem of pearl snaps cracking when laundered. These removable snaps work like buttons in a buttonhole and are completely removable, like a tuxedo-shirt stud. Examples are fairly rare. The demise of removable snaps at Rockmount came about when Jack dropped one at home while removing them for laundering. It rolled behind a wardrobe never to be found again. He discontinued them out of concern that customers would expect free replacements.

Left: Rockmount Ranch Wear, women's plaid cotton shirt, 1940s. The "holy grail" of the earliest Rockmount shirts, this new/old shirt is very rare and features gold piping and matching shank buttons, a long contoured collar, embroidered arrow smile pockets, and front yokes. The star stamp on the collar indicates it was a factory second. Courtesy of Rockmount, Denver, Colorado.

Buttons/Snaps

Closures are a primary design element distinguishing Western from conventional shirts. Few of the earliest Western shirts, from the 1900s to the '20s, survive. We mainly know about them from rodeo photos. Some had huge one-inch sew-through buttons. This element was likely taken from women's wear. They were difficult to button but created a distinctive look.

Shank buttons are a strong design element distinguishing the look from common sew-through buttons. They were in use by the 1930s. Most were Bakelite (a hard resin) or natural shell. They are domed with a sew-through shank. Shank buttons went out of use by the early 1950s, giving way to snaps.

Most companies used variously shaped snaps through the 1950s and '60s. Every shape requires special machinery with specific tool dies to attach them. This means there is a significant start-up cost to use snaps in production. Most companies stopped using any shape but round since the 1960s. Rockmount, the one exception, has kept its signature "Diamond" snap in production.

Jack A. Weil of Rockmount is widely credited as having made the first commercially produced shirts with snaps. Why use snaps? Jack points to the practical "breakaway" feature, where snaps release if the shirt gets caught on a fence, saddle horn, or whatever. Another practical element: no need for a cowboy to be particularly adept with a needle and thread to sew on lost buttons. Most importantly, snaps have a distinct look, and a distinct look was what cowboys wanted, to differentiate themselves from city slickers.

The first shirt snaps were an open-ring type, similar to contemporary diaper snaps. "These shirts sold okay," Jack recalls, but very few were produced, with few or any surviving.

During the war, snaps were unavailable, so Western shirts were made with buttons. Once the war ended, Jack used flat, round enamel snaps, originally created to be used on gloves. They were the earliest snaps used in abundance for commercially made shirts and they came in a range of colors and could be coordinated with the shirt. A number of brands used them in the 1940s and '50s.

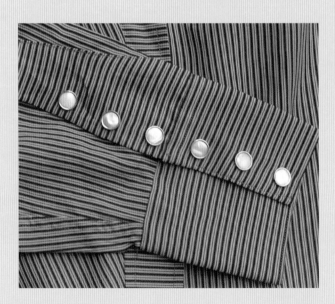

Below: Rockmount Ranch Wear, men's rayon blend cord stripe, 1940s. Features early mother-of-pearl snaps, shotgun cuffs, a tail size stamp, and tail gussets. Courtesy of Rockmount, Denver, Colorado.

Left: Miller Stockman Supply Co. catalog, 1949. Rockmount made the floral embroidery featured at bottom left. The only known surviving example is in Rockmount's collection, shown on page 9. Courtesy of Jack A. Weil, Denver, Colorado.

Pearl snaps are what we normally think of when we talk about snaps. Genuine mother-of-pearl is the smooth pearly lining in oyster and abalone shells. Shell buttons have been used in clothing for centuries and continue to be used today. Most of them are handmade in Asia. The "pearl" snap was adapted from pearl buttons and came into commercial use shortly after World War II. They have beautiful, unique color and luster. The problem with real shell, however, is that it cracks when pressed during laundering.

Synthetic snaps were introduced in the early 1950s as an alternative to the cracking-prone natural shell. Modern snaps are often called "pearl," but that is a misnomer. (For that matter many people mistakenly call snaps "pearl buttons," a holdover from earlier times.) Scovill and Rockmount collaborated to make the first synthetic snaps. Rockmount supplied Scovill with synthetic shank buttons. Scovill removed the shank nub, then set it in a metal rim. Later, Jack developed modern inserts with Rochester Button of Rochester, New York, to be used by Scovill. He did not patent pearl snaps because he wanted them to become the standard of Western shirts. No one company, he reasoned, could achieve that goal on its own.

Although the first snaps were round, snaps came in a variety of shapes and colors. By the late 1940s natural shell became available in a hex shape with nickel or gilt rims. Hex snaps were followed by the diamond shape with nickel and gilt rims. While the hex shape went out of favor in the 1950s, diamond snaps have been in continuous use by Rockmount since their introduction, and imported shirts with hex snaps are being made again.

The front treatment along the snap/button line is a good indicator of age. The earliest shirts, until the late 1940s, typically did not have a top center pleat. They were top-stitched with a simple turn-under. This is because buttons and button-holes require only a single-ply, or better, a double-ply of fabric, to hold securely, but snaps require triple-ply or they tear out. So with the advent of snaps, it became necessary to use a pleated front on Western shirts. In older shirts the front center is a separate pleated strip. Rockmount used the top center pleat on both the lower and top plies of their shirts until the mid-1990s. Automation enabled them to more efficiently sew the top center from a single piece of fabric in one operation. The automatic bottom-ply hem, likewise, had the fabric turned under twice, creating three plies without a pleat. This minor design change saved four operations per shirt.

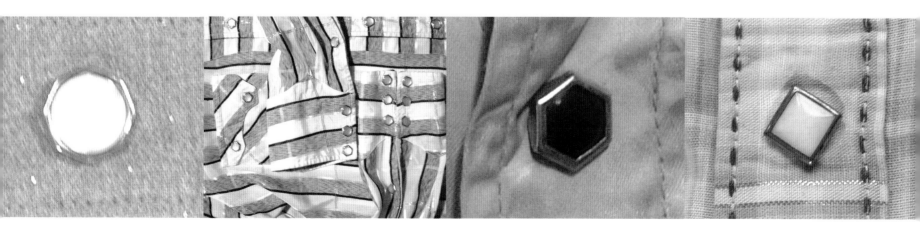

Above, from left to right: Rockmount Ranch Wear, Scoville gilt/mother-of-pearl hex snap, 1950s. Courtesy of Rockmount, Denver, Colorado.

Levi Strauss & Co. grey satin stripe men's shirt, 1950–'60s. Synthetic hex snaps, French-style single-point cuff with duo-stud snaps, and contoured pocket flaps. Courtesy of Ronny Weiser, Las Vegas, Nevada.

Trail Ridge Western Wear, Rau Nickel Black hex snap, 1960s. Courtesy of Ronny Weiser, Las Vegas, Nevada.

Rockmount Ranch Wear, Scovill gilt white diamond snap, 1950s. Courtesy of Rockmount, Denver, Colorado.

As for colors, enamel snaps could be made in any color to coordinate with the fabric. Mother-of-pearl, the most beautiful of snaps, is naturally iridescent. Synthetic snaps can be dyed in a variety of colors too. Traditionally, white synthetic snaps are most common, followed by black or smoke. A number of companies make snaps. The main original brands were Scovill's "Gripper," Rau's "Klik-it" and Dot's "Snappers." Today they have been copied in Asia.

In the aftermath of the Urban Cowboy, many companies dropped snaps in favor of buttons, a new look. Rockmount resisted that trend, continuously using snaps for sixty years, longer than any other brand. They felt that snaps are integral to Western design and that dropping them ran the risk of losing the Western market permanently to other looks.

When talking about collectible vintage shirts, those with snaps are considered classic and the most popular. Although earlier shirts with buttons predate snaps and are rare, they are less expensive in the collector market. Similarly, post–Urban Cowboy shirts with sew-through buttons are not collectible. They are commonly found in thrift stores—cheap and plentiful.

Clockwise, starting with top left:
N. Turk, blue enamel snaps, 1940s. Courtesy of Scott Corey, Santa Fe, New Mexico.

Rockmount Ranch Wear, brown enamel snaps, 1940s. Courtesy of Rockmount, Denver, Colorado.

Unmarked, diamond black/stippled-gilt snaps, 1960s. A nice double-snap treatment on front center. Courtesy of Ronny Weiser, Las Vegas, Nevada.

Below: Rockmount Ranch Wear, Scovill black/nickel round snaps, 1950s. Courtesy of Rockmount, Denver, Colorado.

Below, top: Tem-Tex, Klik-it white/nickel diamond snap, 1950–60s. Note insert has quarter-round corners. Courtesy of Ronny Weiser, Las Vegas, Nevada.

Below, bottom: Rockmount Ranch Wear, Scovill white/gilt hex snap, 1950s. Note how gilt rim coordinates with decorative saddle stitch. Courtesy of Rockmount, Denver, Colorado.

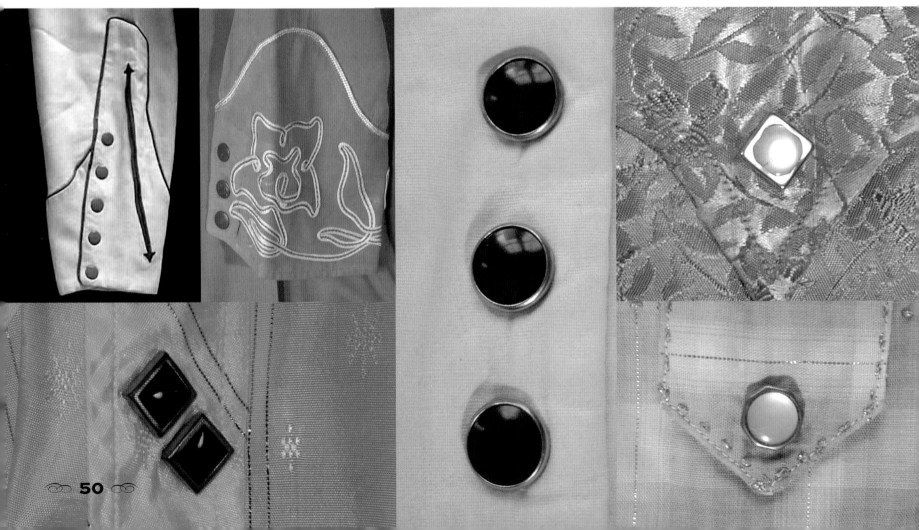

Above: H Bar C Ranchwear, new/old women's plaid two-tone looped fringe, 1970–80s. Courtesy of Scott Corey, Santa Fe, New Mexico.

Above: Hilbilly Westerns, Denver, Colorado, ornate child's two-tone, 1950s, front and back view. Features a long sport collar, a short leather fringe, chenille embroidery, and black enamel snaps. Courtesy of Cowgirls of the West Museum, Cheyenne, Wyoming.

Above: Harris Tailoring Co., Fort Worth, Texas, men's two-tone with embroidery and fringe. Features an extremely ornate, unusual set-in appliqué star, two-tone fringe, and piping. Courtesy of the National Cowboy & Western Heritage Museum, Oklahoma City, Oklahoma.

Fringe

Fringe takes its visual cue from the mane of the horse. Fringe is a design element in traditional American Indian fashion, which inspired the fringed buckskin of mountain men. It is thought that Indians noted that the neck of a horse remains dry under its mane in the rain. They adapted this to suit their needs. But the true practical purpose of fringe has long since been obscured by its role as a fashion statement.

Fringe is usually used to accent yokes and sleeves. It comes in a variety of materials and lengths and is made mostly from faux-leather or string.

Right: H Bar C Ranchwear, men's fringe "guitar" pullover shirt, 1950–60s. This new/old shirt features fringe on front, back, and cuffs. Courtesy of Dan Shapiro, Southwest, Ltd., Costa Mesa, California.

Embroidery, Appliqué, Decorative Stitching, and Embellishment

Embroidery is another early design element seen in American Indian fashion. American Indians embroidered with natural materials such as porcupine quills. This embellishment influenced Western design. Flamboyant figures such as Buffalo Bill favored floral embroidery on their buckskins. This affectation was adopted in the fabric shirts of the early movie cowboys in the 1920s, and remains in use to this day.

Companies like H Bar C are famous for their embroideries because they produced them the longest. These consummate expressions of artistry include images of flowers, steers, and broncos. Besides its artistic merits, embroidery on vintage shirts was labor intensive. Although done on machines, it involved considerable handwork.

Frontier, California, men's green wool gabardine with embroidery, 1940–50s, front and back view. Rare label and very unusual double front yoke, piping, red enamel snaps, snap at long contoured collar, reinforced collar band, five-snap shotgun cuff, unusual tail contour, and piped placket at end, neck, and sleeve size tag. Courtesy of Ronny Weiser, Las Vegas, Nevada.

There are many kinds of embroidery in Western fashion. Here are the main examples:

Chenille chain stitching is a heavy, full-coverage embroidery in large motifs. It is sewn one piece at a time. Often it was done on front, back, sleeves, collar, and cuffs. An art largely lost, it is making a comeback today. The originals are highly prized by collectors.

Below: Mayfair, Los Angeles, Beverly Hills, Hollywood, men's two-tone with embroidery, 1940s, front and back views. Features chenille embroidery, piping, "V" smile pockets with sew-on tabs, very early domed snaps, a long contoured collar, six-snap shotgun cuffs, and an unusual tail contour. Courtesy of David Little, Cody Antique Mall, Cody, Wyoming.

Below: Frontex Co., Dallas, men's two-tone gabardine with embroidery, 1940–50s, front and back views. Features a satin-lined inside yoke, enamel snaps, smile pockets with leather tabs, six-snap shotgun cuffs, a very long contoured collar. Courtesy of Aardvark's Odd Ark, San Francisco, California.

Fay Ward Co. Cowboy Tailors, NYC, 1940s. [...]n-made wool gabardine shirt with long fringe, [...]e embroidery, and rhinestones. Courtesy [...]n and Joyce Neiderman, Chicago, Illinois.

Above: Rockmount Ranch Wear, child's saddle club shirt, 1960s. Chenille was used in lettering on Western shirts, as it was on bowling shirts. Rockmount did customizing for saddle clubs and others. Courtesy of Rockmount, Denver, Colorado.

Above: Circle A Western Wear, California, men's wool gabardine, 1940s. A defunct label with fine chenille embroidery. This shirt features smile pockets with embroidered arrows, piping, shotgun cuffs, and enamel snaps. Courtesy of David Little, Cody Antique Mall, Cody, Wyoming.

Above: Unmarked, men's gabardine shirt with bronc and floral chenille embroidery, 1940s. Features a long contoured collar, piping, smile pockets with embroidered arrows, shotgun cuffs, and enamel snaps. Courtesy of Nathalie Kent, Nathalie, Santa Fe, New Mexico.

Shiffley is multi-headed embroidery, highly automated with repetitive patterns such as eyelets. Full lengths of fabric are embroidered at once.

Bonnaz is a trim sewn down in a pattern, often floral.

Right: Rockmount Ranch Wear, women's shiffley embroidered shirt, 1970s. Shiffley is an automated technique also used with linens. It has an eyelet and stitched pattern treatment. Courtesy of Cowboy Story Antiques, Cody, Wyoming.

Middle and far right: Miller Western Wear, men's embroidered rayon lino, 1960s. Features an interesting inside-hanging pocket with the flap over the embroidery. Others would have done a smile pocket but this design was a departure from the earlier design. Courtesy of Ronny Weiser, Las Vegas, Nevada.

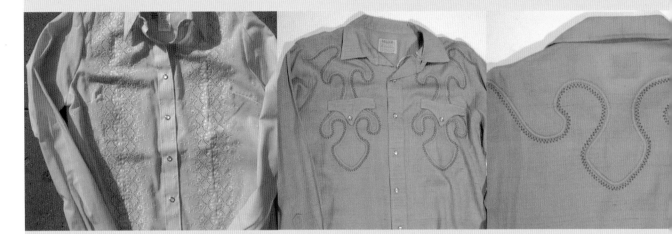

Appliqué is a sewn overlay. It is often used in conjunction with embroidery.

Right: H Bar C California Ranchwear, men's appliqué shirt, 1950s. Features an elaborate white felt floral appliqué with bonnaz embroidery, smile pockets with sew-on tabs, piping, and shotgun cuffs. Courtesy of Bailey's Antiques, Honolulu, Hawaii.

Saddle stitching has been in use for sixty years with a contrasting stitch-space-stitch pattern.

Right: Rockmount Ranch Wear, men's plaid saddle stitch and appliqué, 1960s. Features self-fabric appliqué, smile pockets, and single-point cuffs. This design was reintroduced 2004. Courtesy of Rockmount, Denver, Colorado.

Far right: Rockmount Ranch Wear, men's saddle stitch shirt, 1960s. This model is Rockmount's trademark saddle-stitch design, produced from the 1950s to the 1980s, and again 2004. This version is a white cotton piqué stripe with raglan sleeves and Quarter Horse yokes and pockets. This shirt was embroidered on "Kualoa Ranch" for one of oldest operating cattle ranches in the United States. Courtesy of Island Treasure Antique Mall, Honolulu, Hawaii.

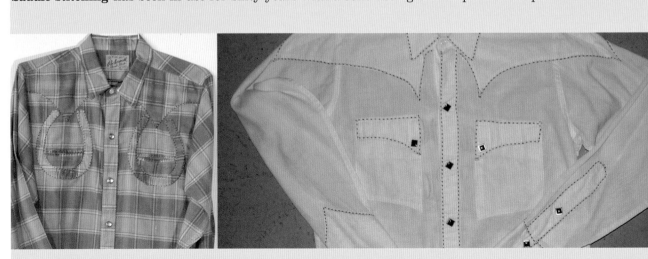

Automatic embroidery, most common today, came into major use in the 1970s. It has a machine-like quality—very consistent, but lacking a hand finish.

Far left: Fenton blue satin men's embroidered shirt, 1970s. Automated embroidery, and shotgun cuffs. Courtesy of/modeled by Barbara Victoria, Cody, Wyoming.

Left: Roundup (Karman) turquoise embroidered shirt, 1960s. New/old factory folded, machine embroidered, and low stitch count. Courtesy of Karman.

Embellishment involves many special treatments, including jewels, studs, rhinestones, and other stones. You can determine aftermarket embroidery and stonework by examining the inside of the garment. If embellished during production, this was usually done on each piece of the shirt separately and the back side is often hidden by inner plies of fabric. If the backside of the embellishment shows it usually means that it was done after the shirt was produced.

Far left, middle: H Bar C Ranchwear, gabardine, 1940–50s. Features embroidery with jewels. Courtesy of Scott Corey, Santa Fe, New Mexico.

Left: Rockmount Ranch Wear, men's model #6801 with saddle stitching, stones, and studs in a starburst pattern. Courtesy of Nicky Paulson.

Above: Levi Strauss & Co., men's floral tie-dye print look, 1960s. Embroidered dragon fly. Courtesy of Nobu Hirota, Johnny Angel/Cactus Blues, Osaka, Japan.

Above: Rockmount Ranch Wear, women's cotton embellished shirt, 1950s, back and front view. This shirt is very collectible, extremely ornate, and unusual because it's more common for the front to be more decorative than the back. Features aftermarket custom saddle club chenille embroidery with rhinestones, a tapered fit, sport collar, single-point cuffs, and diamond snaps. Courtesy of Rockmount, Denver, Colorado.

Pockets

Pockets are like the grill on a car: they define the Western shirt as much as any other element, maybe more.

"Smile" pockets hang on the inside of the shirt, like the front pockets on pants. This may actually be a carry-over from pant design. They are labor intensive to this day and therefore cost more. The construction is complicated with many more operations than a standard "patch" pocket. A pocket pouch is made, the front of the shirt is slit, and the pouch is sewn on the inside. Then the seams where the slit meets the pouch are finished. Sometimes they are piped and have embroidered arrow points on the ends, or a cheaper alternative, sewn-on tabs. They come in a huge array of shapes.

Clockwise from top left:

Tem-Tex, Texas, men's novelty lino with Lurex, 1950s–60s. Features a very stylized "moustache" one-piece yoke pocket flap treatment with triple snaps, and genuine mother-of-pearl snaps. Courtesy of Ronny Weiser, Las Vegas, Nevada.

Herbert, Cincinnati, women's two-tone, 1950s. Unusual features include slanted pocket flaps, and color-coordinated shank buttons in two colors. Also features monogramming, a long contoured collar, and single-point cuffs. Courtesy of La Rosa Vintage Boutique, San Francisco, California.

Ranch-Man Western Wear, Denver, men's plaid, 1950s–60s. Scalloped pocket flaps with pockets cut on the bias, a cheaper alternative to matching fabric pattern which also requires more skill. Also, Rau diamond snaps and small collar. Was originally made by Hilb Co. Ruddock bought the brand in the 1960s.

Rockmount Ranch Wear, men's rayon blend cord stripe, 1940s. Signature Rockmount "sawtooth" style, the longest running shirt design in America. This early version features inside-hanging pockets, genuine mother-of-pearl snaps, six-snap shotgun cuffs, a tail size stamp, and tail gussets. Courtesy of Rockmount, Denver, Colorado.

Rockmount Ranch Wear, women's cotton piqué with saddle stitching, 1950s. Features a sportswear-inspired French front and sport collar, a very tapered fit with four darts, signature Rockmount Quarter Horse pockets and yokes, smoky hex snaps, and single-point cuffs. Courtesy of Rockmount, Denver, Colorado.

Unmarked, men's wool, 1950s. Features arrowhead yokes with four snaps, a short collar, decorative-edge embroidered stitching, a triple-snap front, and brown speckled diamond snaps. Courtesy Ronny Weiser, Las Vegas, Nevada.

Circle A Western Wear, Kohinoor Backbone Fabrics, California, men's two-tone, 1940s–50s. A defunct label with classic smile pockets with embroidered arrows, piping, deep-recess front yokes, shotgun cuffs, and enamel snaps. Courtesy of Kirsten Ehrig (Beverly Hills, California) whose grandfather, David Pollak (Oklahoma) bought it new.

Prior, Denver, men's plaid dobby, 1950s. Another defunct label which produced highly stylized shirts such as this "moustache"-style smile pocket with snap, scalloped yokes, and white diamond snaps. These yokes are unusual with smile pockets. Also, there are no arrows on the ends. Courtesy of Ronny Weiser, Las Vegas, Nevada.

California Ranchwear, houndstooth check, early 1950s. These inverted smile pockets with snap are very unusual but they represent an era in fashion design when being different was what it was all about. Shirt has a highly contoured long collar, slim-fit size tag, self-piping, and no sleeve placket. Courtesy of Ronny Weiser, Las Vegas, Nevada.

Tem-Tex, Texas, men's rayon stripe "The Coloradoan," 1950s. Another inverted smile pocket with triple-snap treatment, long collar, lined inner yoke, slim-fit size, name stamped on collar band, and Rau genuine mother-of-pearl snaps. Courtesy of Ron Weiser, Las Vegas, Nevada.

Flap pockets come in countless styles. The earliest Western flap pocket was made in the 1930s by many companies such as Pendleton, Levi Strauss & Co., and Miller. This style has a single-point flap covering a patch pocket's opening.

The single-point pocket, with the point in the center, is the most common type of Western shirt pocket. They are the easiest to make and more or less generic. They were made by almost every brand and of course remain in production today.

The famous **"sawtooth" pocket** has two points forming a "W." Triple points are rarer, mostly dating from the 1950s. There were many variations on the pointed flap, such as slanted flaps and other shapes.

Jack Frost Woolen Wear, Salt Lake City, wool gabardine, 1930s–50s. A transitional, early Western design with quarter-cut flap pockets, shank buttons, and a long contoured collar. Courtesy of David Little, Cody Antique Mall, Cody, Wyoming.

Rockmount Ranch Wear, women's cotton stripe print, 1954. This zigzag front and sport collar design is taken to the extreme with its stylized upward-pointing patch pocket and snap. Unlike most other styles of the era, this was made exclusively for women. Designers in the 1950s took risks. This is why the golden age overflowed with great design not seen since. Courtesy of Rockmount, Denver, Colorado.

Levi Strauss & Co., men's satin stripe, 1950–60s. Features lots of special treatments including front yokes which run to the tail and Dot hex snaps. Pockets set on the bias use less fabric and are easier to set than pockets that match the body pattern. Courtesy of Ronny Weiser, Las Vegas, Nevada.

Unmarked, men's cotton, 1950s–60s. Features unusual double-stacked snaps on pocket flap, and a short collar. Courtesy of Ronny Weiser, Las Vegas, Nevada.

Panhandle Slim/Lou Taubert Ranch Outfitters, 1950s. A private label with velvet cutaway yokes and hatchet-shaped pockets. Courtesy of Cody Antique Mall, Cody, Wyoming.

Unmarked, men's, 1960s. Rare matching "sawtooth" pocket and cuff treatment and unusual double-snap treatment on front. Pocket pattern matches body, generally a sign of higher quality as opposed to pocket pattern on bias. Courtesy of Ronny Weiser, Las Vegas, Nevada.

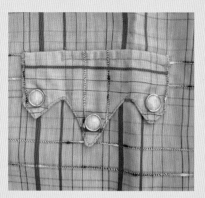

Rockmount Ranch Wear, men's plaid with broken stripe, 1950s–60s. Features mottled round snaps and a "batwing" triple-point pocket flap with inside-hanging pockets—a much more costly treatment requiring more operations and skill than standard patch pockets. Courtesy of Rockmount, Denver, Colorado.

J. C. Penney, Foremost, men's denim work shirt, 1950s. Most brands had long since dropped enamel snaps in favor of synthetic pearl snaps, which cost slightly more but were more fashionable. Denim at this point was strictly utilitarian, so keeping the price low was a major motivation of the manufacturer. Courtesy of Happy Days Vintage, Osaka, Japan.

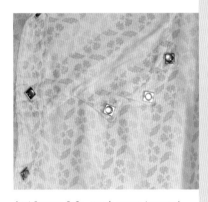

Levi Strauss & Co., men's woven jacquard, 1960s. Features single-piece yoke/pocket flap with triple points set on the bias, and inside-hanging pockets, and Dot diamond snaps with coordinating round turquoise inserts. Courtesy of Ronny Weiser, Las Vegas, Nevada.

Tem-Tex, Texas, men's novelty lino with Lurex, 1950s–60s. Features a very stylized "moustache" one-piece yoke/pocket flap treatment with triple snaps of genuine mother-of-pearl. Courtesy of Ronny Weiser, Las Vegas, Nevada.

Rockmount Ranch Wear, women's Dan River plaid, 1950s. Features a bell-style yoke/pocket flap, gold lurex saddle stitching, gilt diamond snaps, and triple-snap front treatment. Courtesy of Five & Dime Vintage and Rockmount, Denver, Colorado.

California Ranchwear, men's yarn dye stripe, 1950s. Features a single-piece yoke/sawtooth pocket flap, a matched patch pocket, and tapered yoke. Courtesy of Ronny Weiser, Las Vegas, Nevada.

Rockmount Ranch Wear, men's yarn dye shadow plaid dobby by Dan River, 1950s. This early single-piece yoke/tab pocket is scalloped. This is a patch pocket design, unusual in Western shirts. Features a small collar, black hex snaps, and double needling. Courtesy of Rockmount, Denver, Colorado.

Rockmount Ranch Wear, men's cotton jacquard, 1950s. Features a contoured one-piece yoke/tab pocket ending with a "doghouse" point, saddle stitching, a small collar, and black diamond snaps. Courtesy of Rockmount, Denver, Colorado.

Rockmount Ranch Wear, women's yarn dye with lurex stripe, 1950s. The one-piece yoke/tab pocket is combined with a French front and sport collar, a triple-snap front, and gold lurex saddle stitching. Courtesy of Roxanne Thurman, Cry Baby Ranch, and Rockmount, Denver, Colorado.

Rockmount Ranch Wear, complex yarn dye stripe dobby, late 1960s–70s. The one-piece yoke/tab pocket design was the end of the line when it morphed into a double-snap treatment with a much wider and longer tab than its predecessors. Features round snaps and a groovy long collar. Courtesy of Rockmount, Denver, Colorado.

Pockets are like the grill on a car: they define the Western shirt as much as any other element, maybe more.

One-piece, continuous yoke/pocket flaps were made in many designs (see yoke section, pages 43–45, for other shapes.)

Tab pockets for men and women were made in a huge array of variations in the 1950s and into the '60s.

Upward single-point pockets were made for women by Rockmount in the 1950s.

Flapless patch pockets are not usually associated with Western shirts. However, some designers used them in rare examples. (See Prior's early two-tone sportswear-transitional version shown on page 23.)

Later pockets never seemed to have the same creative juice that those from the 1950s Golden Age did, a result of standardization to reduce labor costs.

Left, below: Diamond Shirts, Los Angeles, men's wool gabardine shirt, 1940s. A scarce early label that features a lined collar and triple-point "sawtooth" pocket flaps with patch pockets. Courtesy of Willow Springs Antique Mall, Cody, Wyoming.

Right, below: Rockmount Ranch Wear, men's stripe with lurex, 1950s. Features many special treatments: deeply contoured front yokes with bottom point, Quarter Horse pocket flaps set at a slant with inside-hanging pockets, a six-snap cuff, double needling, and a three-point back yoke. Note how the pocket flap pattern runs across to match the yoke pattern, but the flap is set on angle—an expensive and difficult treatment. Courtesy of Ronny Weiser, Las Vegas, Nevada.

Cuffs

All shirt sleeves have a cuff. Western shirts often have embellished cuffs, whether long sleeve or short sleeve. In long-sleeve design the cuffs always had multiple closures, a major distinguishing characteristic from conventional shirts with one or two buttons. Western shirts have sleeve plackets, as did earlier military uniforms. The multiple buttons and snaps on the cuff may also have come from earlier military jacket or suit jacket design. Western cuffs may have another history altogether: cowboys since the turn of the century sometimes wore removable leather cuffs similar to the gauntlet on gloves. These served a decorative purpose as well as a protective one; many were embellished with tooling and studs. Western cuffs tend to be larger than conventional ones to accommodate the extra fasteners. It may be that because they were tighter fitting, they were less likely to get caught during active use.

The range of cuff designs is as wide as pocket variations. Many of the special treatments require skilled needlework and are not conducive to high automation. There might be only one person in a factory capable of doing certain designs.

Top row from left: Ben The Rodeo Tailor, Philadelphia, men's two-tone heavy gabardine, 1940s. By one of the great early cowboy tailors, it features many special treatments, among them, scalloped shotgun cuffs and downward-pointing smile pockets. Courtesy of Cowboy Story Land & Cattle Co., Cody, Wyoming.

Unmarked, men's gold-lurex stripe, 1960s. Features rare matching "sawtooth" cuffs and pocket treatments. Cuff also has a single-point on top, and the front has an unusual double-snap treatment. Courtesy of Ronny Weiser, Las Vegas, Nevada.

Tanbark, a defunct label, men's woven herringbone, 1940s–50s. Features five mother-of-pearl snaps on contoured shotgun cuffs, and a mitered back yoke. Courtesy of Candy's Vintage, Boulder, Colorado.

Sing Kee, San Francisco, men's wool gabardine, 1940s. Features many very early details, among them: a standard cuff and placket with six early domed pearl snaps, a reinforced sleeve patch, and a tab front with doghouse pleat at bottom. Courtesy of the National Cowboy & Western Heritage Museum, Oklahoma City, Oklahoma.

Bottom row, from left: California Ranchwear, men's rayon gabardine, 1950s. Features a five-snap shotgun cuff and piping. Courtesy of Candy's Vintage, Boulder, Colorado.

Rockmount Ranch Wear, men's rayon blend cord stripe, 1940s. Features shotgun cuffs with six mother-of-pearl snaps. Courtesy of Rockmount, Denver, Colorado.

Circle A Western Wear, Kohinoor Backbone Fabrics, men's two-tone, 1940s–50s. A defunct label featuring pointed and sharply recessed shotgun cuffs with piping and five enamel snaps. Courtesy of Kirsten Ehrig, Beverly Hills, California.

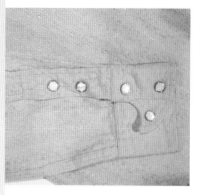

Diamond Shirts, Los Angeles, men's wool gabardine shirt, 1940s. This scarce, early brand features wing-style cuffs and a placket with enamel snaps. Courtesy of Willow Springs Antique Mall, Cody, Wyoming.

Pendleton, men's wool gabardine "Gambler," 1930s. Features four Bakelite cuff buttons. This shirt's transitional style and long, contoured collar predates what we usually think of as Western. Courtesy of Pendleton, Pendleton, Oregon.

Las Vegas Cowboy Joe, men's two-tone/plaid, 1950s. Features a modified shotgun cuff with standard sleeve placket and early, domed sew-through buttons. Courtesy of La Rosa Vintage Boutique, San Francisco, California.

Below: Tem-Tex, Texas, men's novelty lino with Lurex, 1950s–60s. Features a very stylized "shark fin" cuff and placket with five mother-of-pearl snaps. Courtesy of Ronny Weiser, Las Vegas, Nevada.

"Shotgun" cuffs are among the most ornate, a difficult sewing treatment not suitable to mass production. These are single-piece cuffs. Early tailored shirts had very ornate, overlaid cuffs. Some had six or more snaps. Buttons were too cumbersome to use more than three on a cuff, typically. Pendleton, however, did a four-shank-button cuff from the 1930s to the '40s.

Standard, rectangular Western cuffs with three snaps and a snap on the sleeve placket are the most common and easy to make but still require more skill than a conventional shirt. Cuffs were stylized with special treatments to distinguish them.

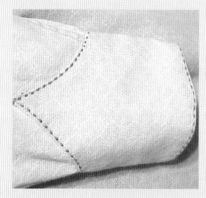

Rockmount Ranch Wear, men's cotton jacquard, 1950s. Features a Rockmount signature cuff design and saddle stitching. Courtesy of Rockmount, Denver, Colorado.

Levi Strauss & Co., men's satin, 1930s–40s. This transitional-style shirt features a winged cuff with mother-of-pearl sew-through buttons, which possibly predate shank buttons and definitely predate snaps. Also has tail gusset. Courtesy of Ron Weiser, Las Vegas, Nevada.

Millie (Miller), women's floral print, 1970s. Features a barrel four-snap cuff. Courtesy of Happy Days Vintage, Osaka, Japan.

Levi Strauss & Co., men's plaid dobby, 1950s–60s. Features a single-point cuff with a duo-stud snap treatment similar to cuff links and French cuffs. Note the interesting Dot brand diamond snap with a round insert. Courtesy of Ronny Weiser, Las Vegas, Nevada.

Sleeve plackets, yet another detail that defines Western design, are not found on all shirts. The sleeve placket has practical and decorative purpose. It reinforces the open seam up the sleeve so that it can be rolled up the arm. It also reinforces a button or snap at the opening that requires more than one ply of fabric. Sleeve plackets are similar to front center plackets. It is an embellishment that may come from military uniform shirt design and continues in use on better dress shirts today.

The basic design is a two-piece rectangular cuff and placket. The most common version is a straight placket with what one Rockmount factory manager called a "dog house" point at the end.

Below: Panhandle Slim, men's wool plaid, 1950s–60s. Features a standard cuff and oversized shotgun-style placket with a quarter-round curve and hex snaps. Courtesy of Boss Vintage, Denver, Colorado.

Below: Ranch-Man Western Wear, Denver, men's cotton plaid dobby shirt, 1950s–60s. Features a highly stylized "fishtail" scalloped sleeve placket and back yoke with decorative embroidered edge, and Rau white marbled snaps. Courtesy of Ronny Weiser, Las Vegas, Nevada.

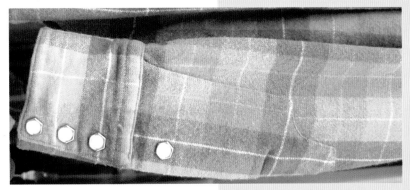

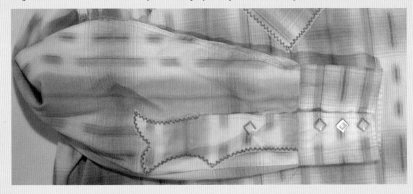

Left: Unmarked, men's two-toned wool gabardine, 1940s. Features very long knife-blade shotgun cuffs, six enamel snaps on each cuff of a different color than those on the front placket, which are tightly spaced. Courtesy of Jerry Glick.

Collars

Men's shirt collars were generally removable until the 1920s but Western shirts had sew-on collars from the beginning. Two kinds of collars characterize Western shirts (and conventional styles): the two-piece construction, whose separate collar band makes the collar stand up (the most common collar), and the one-piece "sport collar," which lays down more casually. The one-piece collar was common in 1950s sportswear. Western women's and kids' shirts utilized sport collars more frequently than did men's. Production costs are cheaper with a one-piece collar, which requires fewer operations. This type of collar often has a single-ply French front. Although simpler to produce than the pleated front, it has a nice lapel-like look. Men's collars are usually slightly longer than women's.

Below: H Bar C, women's two-toned gabardine, 1940s. This rare early label features a long, contoured sport collar, piping, smile pockets with arrow embroidery, and blue Scovill enamel snaps. Courtesy of the National Cowboy & Western Heritage Museum, Oklahoma City, Oklahoma.

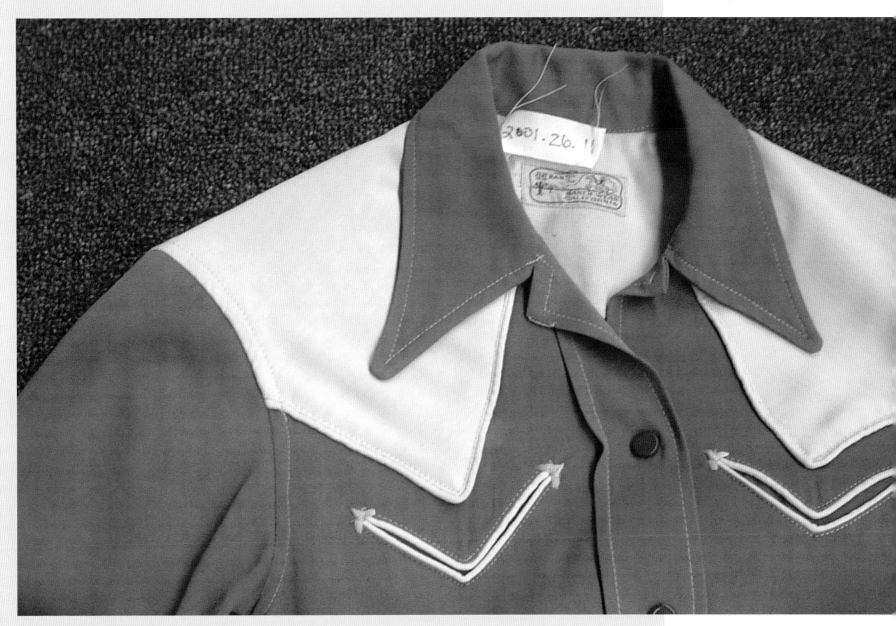

Collar length is a good indicator of when a shirt was made. Collar length in Western shirts has traditionally followed overall fashion trends. During the 1930s and '40s, collars were often about 3 ¹/₂ inches, with very contoured tips; the better ones had removable stays. This requires more operations and a better stay than standard shirts, but it makes a smoother finish when pressed. Today, fine, tailored dress shirts have removable collar stays; Rockmount is probably the only major Western shirt manufacturer with them in its premium makes. Most modern shirts have a sewn-in collar stay—a simpler operation. Collar stays are a feature of two-piece collars, seen in dress shirts, as opposed to more casual sport collars. Women's and children's shirts do not typically have collar stays.

Pendleton, men's wool gabardine, 1930s–40s. Features a transitional style with a long contoured collar, and mother-of-pearl shank buttons. Courtesy of Rockmount, Denver, Colorado.

Vaquero Fashions, Taylor-Berke in California, men's wool suiting gabardine two-tone, 1940s. Features a long, contoured collar and enamel snaps. Courtesy of Ronny Weiser, Las Vegas, Nevada.

Miller Western Wear, men's rayon gabardine, 1930s–40s. Features a long, contoured collar and sew-through buttons, pipings, smile pockets with tabs, and tail gussets. Courtesy of Susan Adams, Richmond, Virginia.

The one-piece sport collar without a collar band was a trend in women's shirts in the 1940s to the '50s. The collar length was about 3 inches until the 1950s, when it was reduced to about 2 ¹/₂ inches. The shortest collars were about 2 inches, during the late 1950s to mid-1960s.

H Bar C, women's stripe, late 1940–early '50s. Features a sport collar with loop and a tapered body. Courtesy of Dan Shapiro, Southwest, Ltd., Costa Mesa, California.

H Bar C, women's, 1950–early '60s. Features a short spread collar. Courtesy of Dan Shapiro, Southwest, Ltd., Costa Mesa, California.

Rockmount Ranch Wear, men's short sleeve, late 1950s–early '60s. Features slanted Quarter Horse pocket flaps, inside-hanging pockets, and diamond snaps. Courtesy of Christopher Anderson, Mendota Heights, Minnesota, and Rockmount, Denver, Colorado.

Collar length became a focal point of the fashion trend of the late 1960s to mid-1970s when collars reached their longest length in all shirts, about 4 inches, an excessive length that represented a changing society's rejection of the conservative 1950s status quo. A veritable "Joseph's shirt of many colors," Rockmount's patchwork shirts for adults and children sported outrageously long collars to complement an in-all-other-ways loud statement (see below).

Trends in the 1980s were a sharp reaction to the excesses of the '70s and collars shortened again to about 2 to 2 ½ inches. These were longer than those of the 1950s but more moderate than those from the '70s. This return to moderation was somewhat sudden, perhaps a reaction against more than just the excesses of collar length but a watershed in overall fashion design. The failure of the Urban Cowboy was addressed by a total revamp of Western shirt design.

Rockmount Ranch Wear, women's print check, 1950s. Features a French-front lapel construction and a "Hi-roll" sports collar popular in sportswear then. Courtesy of Rockmount, Denver, Colorado.

Rockmount Ranch Wear, men's and boys' veritable "coat of many colors," late 1960s. Far out, the longest collar known to man! Courtesy of Rockmount, Denver, Colorado.

Sears, Roebuck and Co., men's denim, 1970s–80s. In contrast to excessively long previous styles, this shirt has a short collar. Courtesy of Cody Antique Mall, Cody, Wyoming.

In fact, the reaction against 1970s design was perhaps too extreme a reduction in collar size; collars have lengthened slightly over time to about 2 ¾ inches for men, which has been holding steady. This is a mid-range length in terms of collar lengths over the decades and will probably last a long time to come.

Collars are an important design element. Contour and edge stitching tell us about the quality of the garment. Wide-gauge stitching is an obvious indicator of cheaper construction. Satin-lined collars were a sign of the finest woolens. Collar shapes and lengths have traditionally changed infrequently because most factories use custom-made metal cutting dies for collars and linings for decades. Today's contemporary automated sewing equipment makes collar design changes difficult too. This is why many vintage remakes have contemporary collars, a clue that helps identify them. Although they are a small feature in terms of the overall shirt, the collar tells a lot about the garment.

STOCKMAN·FARMER
Supply Company

1629-1633 LAWRENCE ST., DENVER, COLORADO

MILLER

largest selection of WESTERN STETSON

CHAPTER 4

MILLER

⚮ WESTERN WEAR ⚮

The story of commercially made Western shirts begins with the first company in the business, Miller and Co. Philip Miller had tuberculosis and came to Denver for the dry air in 1919 when he was in his mid-twenties. The family joke, says daughter Barbara Glazer, was that he came to Denver to die, which he did—sixty years later. Phil Miller's move from New York City, where his brothers had the Miller Brothers Hat Company, eventually established Denver as the center of the Western wear business.

Seymour Simmons, president of Miller from 1972–1989, described the young Phil as a "drummer," or salesman, who brought his brothers' hat line West. The line consisted of dress and Western hats. In those days, Phil would often stay the night with his retailers while traveling. They asked Phil about other things like saddles, jeans—anything they might need. He started with the hat line but soon expanded, eventually wholesaling a full range of products. By 1923, he published his first catalog, The Stockman-Farmer Supply. The catalog would eventually feature shirts, pants, hats, boots, belts, saddles, and accessories under a variety of brands. He sold wholesale to stores and retail to the public, traveling Colorado, Wyoming, Utah, and New Mexico.

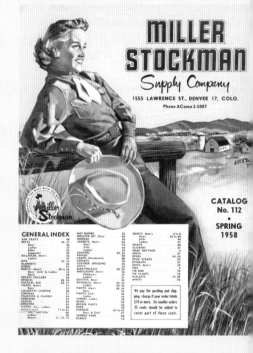

Above: Miller Stockman Supply Co. catalog, 1958. Courtesy of Miller International, Denver, Colorado.

As Miller grew, the firm expanded from jobbing to manufacturing its own brands. Jack A. Weil had experience in manufacturing and sales. He had come to Denver in 1928 to open a sales office for a Chicago firm, the Paris Garter Co. Jack and Phil became friends because of family connections. In 1933, Jack became Phil's partner and together they built the manufacturing side of the business. They developed their own shirt lines and grew the catalog business. They also carried other brands. Jack arranged for Miller to become a regional Levi Strauss agent. When Jack arrived at Miller, the firm's total sales were about $235,000. Five years later, at the height of the Depression, the firm's net profit exceeded its entire 1932 sales. Jack left in 1946 to start Rockmount Ranch Wear Manufacturing Company, but Phil and he remained close, and Miller carried Rockmount shirts in its catalog for decades.

Jack recalls that the first Miller shirts were made by prison inmates in Indiana. It was a

Left: A 1937 catalog cover (reprinted 1972). Courtesy of Miller International, Denver, Colorado.

The Prior Story

Edwin "Eddie" P. Glick was born in 1913 and joined Miller and Co. when he came to Denver in the 1930s. He went to work as a traveling salesman, eventually becoming sales manager. His role expanded to oversee production. He helped set up manufacturing in Japan and Taiwan.

In 1964, Eddie bought one of the oldest names in the Western shirt business, the George W. Prior Company, from Reith Strachan and changed the name to The Prior Company. The company was located on the 1500 block of Wazee Street, the same street that Rockmount and Karman were located on. Prior had begun in the hat business in the 1880s and gone into shirts in the 1940s, after Reith bought the company in the 1930s. According to Eddie's son, Jerry Glick, Reith was ready to retire and might have closed the business had Eddie not bought it.

When Eddie bought Prior, he invited longtime-employee George Hattori to become junior partner, according to George's daughter, Ruth Ann Hattori. George began at Prior in 1953 as a shipping clerk. He worked his way into general management and eventually became a designer in 1960. Eddie and George made a good team. Eddie was strong in sales and marketing, while George knew administration and manufacturing. Ruth Ann Hattori grew up working in the business and joined it full-time in 1977. Ruth Ann was responsible for the Rocky Mountain Jeans line, known as Rockies now.

Prior was sold to Miller in 1981, "completing a perfect circle," according to Seymour Simmons, referring to Eddie's association with Miller in the 1930s. Miller dropped the Prior label shortly after the purchase, but the Rockies label became a major part of their business.

limited selection: solids in basic colors with flap pockets, yokes, and sew-through buttons. (See the navy blue shirt on page 46.) Labor unions stopped interstate commerce of prison goods so Miller was forced to develop new sources in the late 1930s.

Over the years, as the business grew, Miller hired dozens of young men in the Denver area. Many who started while still in high school spent their careers with Miller. For example, Marv Debber and Max Mendelsberg became key employees. Almost everyone in the early Western wear business got their start with Miller. Many of them were very colorful.

• Sam Mandelbaum worked on the wholesale side of Miller, then left in 1948 to start Karman, a major Western firm today.

• Eddie Glick started as a traveling salesman in the 1930s, straight out of high school, then eventually rose to be a vice president of the company. He was known for his fancy duds. Jack Weil recalls Eddie's first sales trip to Salt Lake City. A store owner asked his staff to come see Eddie. "Look at this fancy shirt, collar tips, and boots," he said. "You call yourselves salesmen? Whoever sold him this stuff is a *salesman*!"

Eddie left Miller when he purchased the George Prior company, another early shirt company, in 1964. The Prior company was eventually bought by Miller in 1981.

A 1937 retail catalog cover.
Courtesy of Jack A. Weil,
Denver, Colorado.

A 1949 retail catalog cover. Courtesy of Jack A. Weil, Denver, Colorado.

Some Industry Color

Jack B. Weil recalls one time when Reith was in Jack's office at Rockmount and saw some new sample shirts. One was made out of mattress ticking. Jack A. found that the shirt was no good because the printed stripe flaked off. To make matters worse it had excessive shrinking. So he never produced stock.

Reith later phoned Jack A. "You son of a bitch, why didn't you tell me that stripe shirt was no good?," Reith said. "I made 'em and they all came back!"

Denver became the center of gravity for much of the wholesale side of the Western industry, perhaps because so many people began their careers at Miller. In addition, many Colorado retailers learned the business there too:

• John Nowlen was a mail-order buyer at Montgomery Ward and joined Miller from 1960 to 1970. He left to open his own group of stores, Western Wardrobe, now called High Country Western Wear.

• Lou Bilker worked at Miller after he came home from the U.S. Navy at the end of World War II. His father was Jack Weil's barber, so he sent him to Miller for a job. After Miller, he went to Rockmount, and later opened his own Western store, PMM (Public Merchandise Mart). According to Marvin Parsons of Rockmount, it was always known as PMM; no one called it by its full name. PMM was a group of little stores divided into leased departments. Lou went in on a small basis with Western wear and eventually took over the entire space. PMM was in business over forty years, until the late 1990s.

There have been fourteen corporations under the Miller umbrella over the years. The company is now known as Miller International. One of the old-line names owned by Miller was the retailer and saddle maker Fred Mueller in downtown Denver, now closed. Miller also owned the famous Wrangler store in Cheyenne, Wyoming, which later sold to Corral West in 1965. The Miller Stockman store chain and catalog (successor to Stockman-Farmer Supply Co.), was later sold to Corral West in 1999, who dropped the name and catalog. The final catalog mailing went to over three million customers. Countless millions of Miller catalogs were printed over the years.

Facing: A 1958 retail catalog cover. Courtesy of Miller International, Denver, Colorado.

MILLER STOCKMAN
Supply Company

1555 LAWRENCE ST., DENVER 17, COLO.

Phone AComa 2-5887

"...BRANDING THE WEST WITH THE BEST"

Miller Stockman

CATALOG No. 113
SUMMER — 1958

GENERAL INDEX

ASH TRAYS 57
BELTS 18, 19
   Boys' 40
   Ladies' 19
   Rider 15
   Supporter 15
BILLFOLDS, Men's 15
   Ladies' 15
BITS 50, 51
BLANKETS 45
BOOKS 53
BOOTS—Men's .... 21 to 27
   Boys', Girls' & Ladies' 27
   Shoes 21
BREAST COLLARS 46
BRIDLES 46, 47
BUCKLES, Belt 18, 19
CHAPS, Men's 48
   Boys' 39
CINCHAS 55
COASTERS & GLASSES 57
CONCHAS 56
DRESSES 61
GLOVES 49
HALTERS 47
HAND BAGS, Ladies' 62
HATS, Men's .... 2 to 13
   Boys' and Girls' 40
   Ladies' 62
   Straws 2, 3, 4

HAT BANDS 12
HOLSTER SET, Boys' 40
HONDAS 54
JACKETS, Men's 20
   Boys' 38
   Girls' 38
   Ladies' 64
JUMPERS 14, 15
KNIVES 57
LAMPS, Ornamental 57
LARIATS 54
LEATHER DRESSING 21
LEVI'S 14
MARTINGALES 46, 47
MOCCASINS, Men's 21
   Children's 63
   Ladies' 63
OUTFITS, Boys' 41
OVERALLS, Men's 14, 15
   Ladies' 14, 15
PANTS, Men's 16, 17
   Boys' 41
PANTS, Girls' 38
   Ladies' 60
PURSES, Ladies' 62
REINS 47
REPAIR PARTS 56
ROPE 54
SADDLES .... 42 to 44
   Boys' & Girls' 39
SADDLE PADS 45
SCARFS 28

SHIRTS, Men's .... 30 to 36
   Boys' 37, 38
   Ladies' 30, 31, 58, 59
SKIRTS 60
SLICKERS 15
SNAP BUTTONS 32
SPOTS 55
SPURS 52, 53
SPUR STRAPS 53
STIRRUPS 55
SUITS, Men's 17
TIES 29
TIE BAR 28
TIE CLASPS 28
WALLETS 15, 28
WHIPS 56

We pay the packing and shipping charge if your order totals $10 or more. On smaller orders 35 cents should be added to cover part of these costs.

Enjoy Summer Fun in a Handsome Miller Shirt

Ladies' U-Rollit Bailey Straw — Here's the perfect hat to complete any Western outfit from casual to dress. Sparkling metallic thread and sequins form the band and matching brim edge trim. Low Chute crown and wide brim with hidden wire. Color: White hat with Gold metallic trim.

C518   Sizes: 6⅝ to 7¼   **$7.50**

See Men's Stetson Imperial, pg. 36
See Boys' Straw hats, pg. 38

FAMILY MATCH-MATES — Get set for casual Summer fun in this gay floral print. Washable, all cotton fabric requires little or no ironing. Pointed front and back yokes. Lustrous pearlized snaps. Men's has permanent collar stays and panel back for that trim, Western fit. Boys' has collar stays. Here's a shirt your entire family will go for. Colors: Red, Blue, Gold — all on White grounds.

Men's E5242   **$5.98**   **Ladies' H7272**   **$3.98**
Sizes: 14 to 16½   Sizes: 32 to 38
Sleeves: 32, 33, 34, 35

                                    Boys' J3247   **$3.98**
                                    Sizes: 4 to 16

CATALOG NO. 135
SUMMER 1963

"BRANDING THE WEST WITH THE BEST"

Miller Stockman

MILLER STOCKMAN

1555 LAWRENCE STREET, DENVER 2, COLORADO

Phone 222-5887

A 1963 retail catalog cover. Courtesy of Miller International, Denver, Colorado.

Miller Innovations

In the 1930s Phil Miller saw Tom Mix, one of the first cowboy movie stars, wearing plain shirts. He decided there was a need for real Western shirts.

Phil Miller's son, Ben, joined the company after leaving the U.S. Navy during World War II. He eventually ran the company and was one of the earliest apparel importers, beginning to import shirts in 1954. Seymour Simmons says J. C. Penney Company, Inc., a big Miller account, asked for a boy's shirt to retail at $1.95 and men's at $2.95. This could not be done domestically. Penney said they could do it in Japan. Ben went back to the University of Colorado to learn Japanese. He had interpreters but he preferred to listen to what they were really saying. The Japanese were known to be good at copying things. Miller sent a shirt sample with a hole in the tail so the Japanese factory would not have to pay duty on it. The first stock from Japan came with the same hole in the tail. Despite the faulty start, Miller imported from Japan for a number years. As Japanese costs rose, Miller went to Korea, Taiwan, and other places in search of lower costs.

Ben Miller, like his father, was a true merchandiser. He was involved throughout the operation from product design to sales. He was president from the mid-1950s to 1972.

The company once received a child's shirt accompanied by a complaint that it had worn out. The shirt had been worn by three generations of the family.

Ben's widow, Marianne Cohn, recalled that Miller made shirts in Japan because of the good quality and low prices. They were also their own market. The Japanese wanted Western shirts, so Miller imported shirts from there to sell in the United States and exported American-made shirts to sell in Japan. Marianne recalls a time that the company received a worn-out child's shirt with a note complaining about its quality because it had worn out. The shirt had been worn by three generations of family.

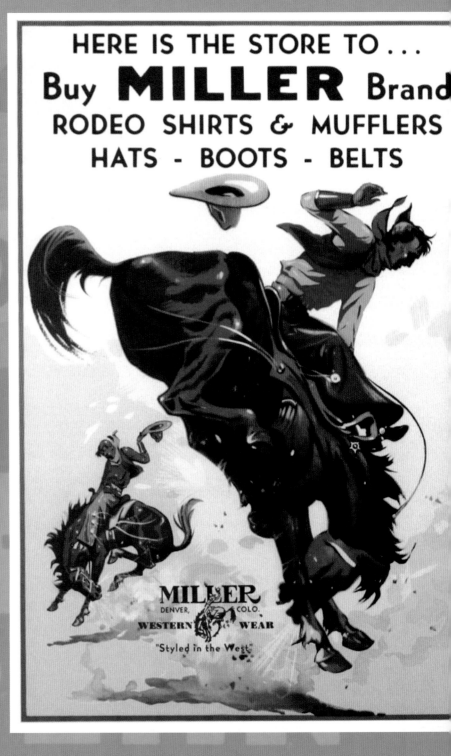

Buy MILLER Brand
RODEO SHIRTS   SCARFS   HATS
VESTS   BELTS   BOOTS
for MEN WOMEN CHILDREN

MILLER
DENVER, COLO.
WESTERN WEAR
"Styled in the West"

You'll Look Well in Western Clothes

Promoting the romance of the West was what made Western wear popular then and now. These posters were printed by Miller in the 1930s for their retail store customers. Courtesy of Miller International, Denver, Colorado.

HERE IS THE STORE TO . . .
Buy MILLER Brand
RODEO SHIRTS & MUFFLERS
HATS - BOOTS - BELTS

MILLER
DENVER, COLO.
WESTERN WEAR
"Styled in the West"

Ron Schmitz started in the retail division of Miller Stockman in 1976, and became president of Miller International in 1999. He points out that Miller was a pioneer in vertical operations with manufacturing, wholesale, and retail divisions. Today the company is focused on merchandising and wholesale distribution; the factories and retail are gone.

Seymour Simmons recalled that they had a licensee that produced shirts under the Miller brand in Australia. The Australian company told Miller that in Australia all Western shirts were called "Miller" because at the time they were the dominant brand.

Miller continues to play an important role in the Western industry. The company developed on the basis of a friendship. That is a legacy that exists to this day. According to Ron Schmitz, "What I like best about the Western industry is that deals get done with a handshake."

For Collectors of Miller ★★★★★★★★★★★★★★★★★★★★★★★★

Label Dating Guide

The early Miller labels are woven and sewn on all sides. Labels from the 1970s and '80s are zigzag-stitched on the sides. Some of the early imports have glued-in labels.

—Red "MILLER," red bronc/blue cowboy, blue Denver, Colorado: 1930s.

—Brown scrolls, "MILLER WESTERN WEAR, Denver, Colorado," on tan: 1930s to the '60s.

—Green "MILLER, Denver, Colorado," brown bronc rider, mountain and cactus on tan: 1950s.

—Red "MILLER, Ride 'em Cowboy, Denver, Colorado": 1960s.

—Stacked, triple "Miller" in red, yellow, and pink: 1970s.

—Pink "Millie," gold horse: women's wear, 1970s.

—Miller flag motif in red, white, and blue: 1980s.

★★★★★★★★★★★★★★★★★★★★★★★★★★★★★★★★★★★

Left: Fred Mueller retail catalog, 1966. Fred Mueller was a saddle maker and retail-store owner in downtown Denver, in business from 1891 to the 1970s. Jack A. Weil recalls selling Miller apparel to Mueller and buying Mueller's saddlery and tack for Miller. Jack helped Mueller develop their own catalog business. Eventually Miller bought Mueller, later dropping the name when the store became Miller Stockman, now defunct. Courtesy of Miller International, Denver, Colorado.

Rockmount
Ranch Wear
DENVER   COLO.

Styled in the West by Westerners

CHAPTER 5

★ ★ ★ ★ ★

ROCKMOUNT

 RANCH WEAR MFG. CO.

Rockmount Ranch Wear Mfg. Co. was the first company to commercially make shirts with snaps. Likewise, it was the first company to go into business with the express purpose of manufacturing Western shirts, and Jack A. Weil, who founded it, has been described as the Henry Ford of Western shirts. Jack's innovations in the design and production of Western shirts helped launch an industry and define a lifestyle.

His life-long career in apparel began during World War I. He was in high school and worked part-time at the D. S. Bernstein Overall Factory, in Evansville, Indiana. What he learned on the factory floor as a teenager directly impacted his future career and the direction of Western fashion.

Jack moved to Denver, Colorado, in 1928 with his young wife, Bea. He opened a sales office for A. Stein & Co., a Chicago firm that manufactured Paris Garters. In 1933, he went into business with his friend Phil Miller at Miller & Co., the earliest Western wear manufacturer. Together they built a company that prospered despite, and perhaps because of, the Depression.

Jack and Phil developed a new style of shirt for their farming and ranching customers that came to be known as *Western wear*. An American phenomenon, Western wear gained popularity first by helping people in the West distinguish themselves sartorially from the conventional fashion of the rest of the country. People could escape the malaise of the Depression by identifying with real cowboys, as well as the mythic ones on the silver screen. Jack and Phil hit a gold vein. They found a rural market that could afford Western clothing despite the worst economic conditions in modern history. The counter-cultural element of Western fashion extended to the industry itself, which thrived during later recessions. Western fashion simply made people happy in an otherwise dark time. Jack and Phil launched a new look, America's only truly original fashion: Western wear.

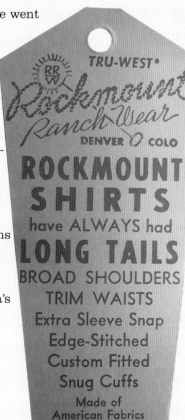

Shirt hang tag, 1970.
Courtesy of Rockmount,
Denver, Colorado.

Left: *Rockmount's signature bronc logo, here silk screened on a retail store counter sign from the 1940s. Only seven such signs are known to exist. Courtesy of Rockmount, Denver, Colorado.*
Rockmount Ranch Wear Mfg. Co. owns the exclusive right to this and all other Rockmount designs. Reproduction is prohibited without express written permission of Rockmount. Tru-West and Rockmount are Registered Trademarks under the laws of the U.S.A. and foreign countries.

*Right: Wear Magazine, 1959.
Courtesy of Rockmount, Denver,
Colorado.*

Jack is known for being the first manufacturer to use snaps in shirts. "We Put the Snaps in Western Shirts" is a longtime Rockmount slogan. His snap shirt design predated World War II but did not go into significant production until the war ended and manufacturing returned to a peace-time economy. When he first approached Scovill to make snaps for shirts, they initially declined because it was a "misapplication." Today, Rockmount is their oldest customer.

WE HAVE NO QUARREL WITH THOSE WHO SELL FOR LESS... THEY SHOULD KNOW WHAT THEIR PRODUCT IS WORTH. BUYING "QUALITY MER-CHANDISE" is like buying oats. If you want nice, clean, fresh oats, you must pay a fair price. However, if you can be satisfied with oats that have already been through the horse... they come a little cheaper.

ROCKMOUNT RANCH WEAR

*An early calling card for salesmen, 1950s.
Courtesy of Rockmount, Denver, Colorado.*

Jack's responsibilities included design, manufacturing, and advertising. He loved to design and produce ornate, high-quality shirts. Shortly after World War II ended, he left Miller and founded Rockmount Ranch Wear Mfg. Co.

There he originated many elements of classic, Western shirt design including the slim fit, front yokes, "sawtooth" pockets, and various fancy cuff treatments. His designs became fashion standards. Yokes accentuate a man's broad shoulders. Snaps were a "breakaway" feature so the shirt would not get caught on a saddle or steer horn. Most importantly, these new shirts gave the cowboy a fashion identity. The entire Western look was meant to be distinct from conventional boxy shirts of the era. Cowboys wanted to be different from city slickers. In the tradition of the rugged individualism key to cowboy ethos, Western clothing helped them define their special identity.

Much as Henry Ford brought his product to the public by making it affordable by innovating efficient manufacturing techniques, Jack developed ways to make expensive-looking Western clothes more affordable. The earliest Western shirts were expensive—custom-made by tailors for celebrities. It is one thing to design nice shirts but something entirely different (and complicated) to engineer their efficient production. Jack was a driving force to that end.

The big chains demanded cheaper goods. Jack had never liked the discount chain-store business, which was primarily motivated by price. His target market then, same as today, was better specialty stores, not the discounters. His original commitment to small, locally owned businesses remains central to Rockmount's philosophy. So rather than be dependent on them, Jack built distribution through independent retailers across the country. He felt a healthy economy depended on small scale, grassroots business. This was also how he could avoid compromising quality and design. Whereas other manufacturers discounted their prices to the chains and charged higher prices to smaller stores, Jack maintained a one-price label. His "one price" policy supported small retailers. Why, he figured, should the little guy pay more, in effect subsidizing the discounters? He felt he could sell one hundred independents the same amount as he could sell to a one-hundred-store chain, and he gave credit the old-fashioned way—with a handshake.

The process of building a market beyond the West jelled in the mid-1950s. Jack A.'s son, Jack B., joined the company in 1954. He began in sales and went on the road, introducing Western fashion to Americans east of the Mississippi. He eventually took over Rockmount's design function, handling it for over thirty-five years. Jack B.'s innovations include the concept of matching clothes for men, women, and children. His navy Rockmount Ranch Wear cuff tab was trademarked in 1975. At that time, Levi Strauss & Co. held the one and only other label-positioning trademark. Perhaps his proudest accomplishment was to help popularize Western wear nationwide.

PROFILE—Three Generations

The Rockmount Ranch Wear Manufacturing Co. of Denver was founded twelve years ago by Jack A. Weil who has been associated with the Western Wear business since the early 1930's. His son, Jack B. Weil, now 30, entered the business after his discharge from the army in 1954.

The elder Mr. Weil is a pioneer in the Western Wear field, and has seen many of the innovations of past years now fully accepted. With others he is responsible for the present universal use of the pearl snap button on western shirts, and introduced into the industry the idea of tailored Western Wear for general sports wear, styling the shirts away from the early standard satin-piped, denim, and plain gabardine, which were largely the only factory-made shirts of the day.

One of the original ideas was the matching ladies' and men's shirts for general wear with the ladies' shirts having styled collars for casual or "rodeo" wear, and many of the basic patterns in use today for the Western shirt were originally cut by Mr. Weil.

He is recognized as a leader in the field with constantly new yoke styles and fabrics coming out of the Rockmount factories with currently over 100 shirt styles representing several thousands of dozens of shirts in stock for "same day" shipment.

The company on its formation set several sales policies from which it has never varied. All merchandise, which includes a complete line of wool-felt hats, straws, buckles, belts, ties, accessories, as well as shirts carry the one label ROCKMOUNT. The business is entirely wholesale with no retail sales, nor any direct-to-consumer affiliates, with sales to independent merchants only.

Rockmount Ranch Wear is a large but personalized business with either father or son always available to talk business or just visit with anyone who comes in to the downtown Denver

Third generation Steven with his grandfather Jack A. Weil, and be-whiskered dad Jack B. Weil; the beard is temporary in honor of Colorado's Centennial. Young Steven, 18 months, is already a model and "showpiece" in his western outfit. This picture was taken in the sample room of the Rockmount Ranch Wear business office at 1636 Lawrence St. in Denver, Colorado.

business office. Both take part in civic affairs. Jack Jr. is a part of the welcoming committee of the Colorado Centennial celebration, and Jack Sr. this year is Chairman of the Colorado Apparel Manufacturers of the Colorado Centennial Commission, and is also vice-president of the Market Development Committee of the Denver Chamber of Commerce.

Between the two Jacks, they are personal friends of the majority of their customers, and while the total number of customers is imposing, and still growing, their ambition is to be personally acquainted with all of them. With third generation Steven already making his share of friends they may well get it done.

Jack B.'s son, Steve, grew up in the business. He worked his way up through the company, and in the late 1980s, went into design, building on the foundation laid by his grandfather and father. In 1988 he introduced relaxed-fit shirts, now an industry standard, to Western fashion.

The Weil family has seen the Western business evolve from regional to national to international in three generations. Rockmount is the last of the original Western apparel manufacturers to produce most of its products in the United States. Today, the Rockmount brand is sold by 2,000 retailers worldwide, from saddle shops in Montana to high-fashion boutiques in New York, Paris, Tokyo, and other fashion capitals.

See Pages 19, 41 & 42 for Additional ROCKMOUNT RANCH WEAR

Wholesale catalog page, 1950s. Courtesy of Rockmount, Denver, Colorado.

*Jack A. never liked colored snaps
because of the difficulties they created
during manufacturing. A stray one
always got mixed with another color
on the same shirt. Rockmount discontinued colored snaps in the 1950s but
reintroduced them in the mid-1990s.*

Rockmount in the Media

While the movies influenced Western fashion originally, today Rockmount influences fashion in the movies. Rockmount shirts have been worn by Hollywood stars in dozens of films including, Nicholas Cage in *Red Rock West*, Meg Ryan and Dennis Quaid in *Flesh and Bone*, Woody Harrelson in *The Cowboy Way*, Aidan Quinn in *Practical Magic*, *Insomnia*, and *Bandits*, Chris Cooper in *Silver City*, and will be worn in Ang Lee's *Brokeback Mountain*.

Rockmount's TV credits include features on CNN, Discovery's Travel Channel, The Western Channel, and a 2004 episode of *The Sopranos*.

Rockmount is also popular in the music business and has been worn by, among others, Elvis Presley, Bob Dylan, Johnny Cash, Roseanne Cash, Don Henley, Robert Plant, Hank Williams III, Alan Jackson, and Ronnie Dunn.

Whenever Western apparel makes the news, Rockmount is prominently featured. Rockmount has appeared in the *New York Times*, *Wall Street Journal*, *Esquire*, *Vogue*, *Gentleman's Quarterly*, the *Denver Post*, *Rocky Mountain News*, and *Westword*.

Rockmount headquarters remain in a historic landmark building at 1626 Wazee in lower downtown Denver, where the company has been since 1946. Rockmount is one of three remaining early mercantile businesses in "LoDo's" historic district. Its lobby is a museum and store, reflecting Western wear's history and its future. The museum has a large collection of vintage Rockmount and Western memorabilia.

Below: Rockmount made thousands of these very collectible six-foot, wood, silk screened signs for retailers, 1950s. Courtesy of Rockmount, Denver, Colorado.

Rockmount's Challenges

Typically, the start-up of a business is its greatest challenge. However, once established there are far greater challenges to survival. Family businesses often cannot overcome the difficulty of making the transition from one generation to the next. That said, Rockmount survived a number of downturns that brought other firms down.

Jack A.'s midwestern sensibilities saved the ranch during the Urban Cowboy fad of the 1970s, the beginning of the Western industry's first boom-and-bust cycle. At that time, Rockmount stopped taking orders from new customers so it could satisfy existing ones. Interest rates were high, major department stores were slow to pay. Jack A. laid down the law and said no shipments to slow-paying major department stores. While Rockmount made huge investments in inventory, it did not commit to long-term expansion as did other companies, which were bankrupted when the fad ended. It took years to move the excess inventory, but the company persevered.

The current deluge of cheap, foreign imports has been Rockmount's greatest challenge since starting in business. NAFTA decimated the U.S. textile and apparel manufacturing industries; less than five percent of them survive. The loss of domestic sources makes operating in the United States more difficult.

Rockmount has always believed that Western clothing, as classic American fashion, should be made in America. They fought cheap, unfair imports from countries that pay workers per day what is paid per hour in the United States, a moot point today. Rockmount's distinct identity is strengthened now as the last original domestic manufacturer of Western apparel. Exclusively a domestic manufacturer for fifty years, some items simply cannot be made in the United States today. Rockmount imports a small percentage of its products.

Back in the '30s, Jack A. started in business by taking out ads in country newspapers. Today, the Web has leveled the playing field for small businesses in their struggle against mass marketers; Rockmount reaches the world one person at a time with a mouse click. Enter its office today and see 103-year-old Papa Jack hard at work behind his computer.

Left: Mr. Walnut Head, a Rockmount sales gimmick from the late 1940s–50s, preceded Toy Story's Woody by decades. Jack A. Weil recalls having these made by an immigrant shoemaker in Cheyenne named Goldstein. Goldstein later moved to downtown Denver at 15th and Arapaho Streets. The doll was made from leather washers cut from scrap strung on wire. Thousands were sold, some with miniature saddles and horses. This one was found by Reed Weimer and Chandler Romeo. Courtesy of Rockmount, Denver, Colorado.

For Collectors of Rockmount ★ ★ ★ ★ ★ ★ ★ ★ ★ ★

Label Dating Guide

—Rockmount labels are like an artist's signature. They are expensive multi-colored woven labels. All are fully edge-stitched on all four sides, never glued.

—Rainbow "Original Model": 1946–early '50s. Size printed on inside collar band or shirttail. This predates advent of size tags, until 1954.

—Rainbow "Washable," size tag sewn below label: 1950s.

—Rainbow "Wrinkle-shed—It's a Dan River Fabric": 1950s.

—Rainbow "Custom Fitted": 1950–1975.

—White/navy "Custom Fitted" replaces the old rainbow label with a new color scheme to update brand: 1975–89.

—Navy "RR/W" cuff tab introduced on right sleeve and trademarked: 1975.

—White/navy byline "Made in U.S.A." replaces "Custom Fitted" due to advent of relaxed fit: 1989–present.

—Rainbow "Made in U.S.A." reintroduced for Rockmount's vintage collection and premium fabrics: 1992–present.

Snaps and Buttons

—Bakelite shank buttons predate snaps: 1946.

—Open-ring snaps were the first snaps Rockmount put on shirts, as an experiment, but they were not decorative enough, so were dropped.

—First production of enameled snaps: 1946.

—First use of round, genuine mother-of-pearl snaps: late 1940s.

—Duo-stud snap with genuine mother-of-pearl: late 1940s–early '50s.

—Synthetic snaps: early 1950s–present. Original modern inserts developed with Rochester Button of Rochester, New York, to be used by Scovill.

ad in snap fasteners is the 'GRIPPER' Brand. There's a
' 'em you can see for yourself. Like how the ribs on the
nap Fasteners stronger—they'll last as long as the shirt
pearl caps on GRIPPER Snap Fasteners make western
Real style. They won't rust, or get out of shape in the
to appreciate things like that. Women, too, of course. We
olks who sell garments with GRIPPER Snap Fasteners.''

Snap
rib socket—
A product of
makers of

PEARLIZED CAP. One of
the many decorative caps
from the complete line of
GRIPPER Snap Fasteners.
They add fashion and sale-
ability to your lines.

RADIAL RIB SOCKET. Ribs
strengthen the socket just
as spokes strengthen a
wheel. Rolled lip and deep-
er socket mouth mean firm,
consistent snap action.

Left: Scovill Gripper co-op ad with Rockmount, 1950s. Jack A. Weil put Scovill in the shirt-snap business. Scovill advertised with Rockmount products for decades. Courtesy of Rockmount, Denver, Colorado.

s by ROCKMOUNT RANCHWEAR
Denver, Colorado

—Hex-snap, and nickel- and gilt-rim snaps: late 1940s–50s.

—White nickel and gilt diamond snaps: early 1950s to present.

—Black nickel and gilt diamond snaps: early 1950s, reintroduced in mid 1990s.

—White and black round snaps: 1950s, reintroduced in late 1990s.

Sizing

Traditionally, Western shirts were all slim fitting. This changed in the late 1980s. Slim-fit sizing was the only fit used by Rockmount until the advent of relaxed fit in 1988. Rockmount continues to offer slim fit in various designs.

—Men's slim-fit neck sizing 14 to 20 inches and sleeve sizing 32 to 36 inches: since 1946.

—Women's bust sizes 30 to 44 inches: since 1946.

—Children's age sizes 0/1 to 16: 1957. (Jack B. introduced size 0/1 when Steve was born.)

—Relaxed fit, which now accounts for most of current production: 1988–present.

Collars

Lengths are for men's shirts unless otherwise indicated. Women's are usually ¼ inch shorter.

—1940s: 3 ½ inches, very contoured, some with removable stays.

—1950s: women's sport collar without collar band, 1 ½ inches.

—Late 1960s: men's collar, 2 inches.

—Late 1960s–70s: 4-inch collar.

—1980s to present: 2 ¾-inch collar.

—1999: reintroduced 3 ½-inch vintage collar from 1940s for select vintage remakes.

—2000: dress-shirt collar with removable collar stays in premium makes and fabrics for the smoothest ironing.

Design features

—YOKES: First shirts with front yokes: 1946. Yoke designs include standard single-point, Quarter Horse point offset, double-point, yoke/pocket in one, etc.

—DOUBLE NEEDLING: Side gussets, side seam, and arm hole double needling: 1940s. Discontinued when Singer developed a lock-stitch serger, adopted in the early 1950s. Double needling was reintroduced in the late 1980s.

—COLLARS: Edge-stitched: 1946 to present.

—SHIRTTAILS: All shirttails topstitched with rolled hem: 1946 to present.

—POCKETS: "Sawtooth" pocket flap introduced 1946 to present, the longest-running shirt in America, Western or otherwise. The smile pocket with embroidered arrows, a finer finish than sewn-on tabs, was produced from 1946 through the mid '60s. They were reintroduced in the mid '80s and have been produced ever since. The Quarter Horse pocket, double-point pocket flaps, yoke/pocket and other special treatments were introduced in the 1950s. Pocket flap pen slot: 1946 to present.

—SADDLE STITCHING: Introduced in 1946, a signature treatment.

—CUFFS: Standard, shotgun, single-point on top, single-point on side, etc.

—FIT: Introduced relaxed fit to the Western shirt industry in 1988, eventually an industry standard. French fronts with sport collars were used in some women's shirts in the 1940s to the '50s, and have been used again since the late '90s. Most shirts had separate top-center plackets on both the top and underside of the shirtfront from 1946 to 1996. The underside had a separate top-center pleat sewn to the front of the shirt from top to bottom. Three layers of fabric are needed to hold the snaps securely. This design was dropped in 1996 in favor of a hemmed, turn-under design that is simpler and leaves a smoother finish underneath. Two top-center plackets distinguish original designs from later remakes.

★ ★

CHAPTER 6

THE
H BAR C
STORY

H Bar C was an equestrian apparel firm that later made Western shirts. The story began in 1897 when Samuel Christenfeld started making English riding britches labeled "Tailoring by Christenfeld, in Brooklyn, NY." In 1906, he formed a partnership with M. Halpern called Halpern and Christenfeld. This was the origin of the H Bar C brand.

Halpern died in 1929 but his brand continued. Christenfeld had five sons in the business: Bernie, Seymour, Stanley, Leonard, and Paul. Bernie was the driving force of the Western side of the business, which was primarily pant and coat related in the early years. By the late 1940s he wanted to expand, so he went to Rockmount to have his first Western shirts made. Accordingly, some of the early H Bar C shirts were very similar to those made by Rockmount.

H Bar C later operated a factory in downtown Los Angeles, a small operation where they did special treatments and custom work. There, Seymour Christenfeld worked with Nudie, the famous Hollywood custom tailor, and H Bar C made some of Nudie's production styles. In 1972, the factory was moved to Gardena, California. These California-made H Bar C shirts are the most collectible.

The California operation was oriented toward special treatment styles, not basics. The basic shirts were mostly produced by a private contractor, The Hill Co. of Fort Smith, Arkansas. This contractor was in business for about fifty years before it closed in 1996, a casualty of NAFTA.

Based in New York, H Bar C later opened offices in Denver and Los Angeles. Seymour opened the L.A. office in 1936. They later introduced the H Bar C/California Ranchwear label. Catering to Hollywood, they supplied clothes for the likes of Gene Autry, Roy Rogers, and John Wayne.

Below: Seymour Christenfeld's business card. Seymour built and ran H Bar C/California Ranchwear for more than fifty years. Courtesy of Dan Shapiro, Southwest, Ltd., Costa Mesa, California.

SEYMOUR CHRISTENFELD

H BAR C RANCHWEAR

CALIFORNIA RANCHWEAR, INC.
14600 SOUTH MAIN STREET
GARDENA, CALIF. 90248
(213) 532-8980
FROM L.A. CALL 321-6833
101 WEST 21ST STREET
NEW YORK, N.Y. 10011
1430 - 23RD STREET
DENVER, COLO. 80205

Above: The H Bar C office and warehouse was located at 1430 23rd Street, Denver, from 1960–1996. Courtesy of Dan Shapiro, Southwest, Ltd., Costa Mesa, California.

Above: *H Bar C, women's sleeveless shirt ad, 1950s. Note the triple-snap front treatment. Courtesy of Dan Shapiro, Southwest, Ltd., Costa Mesa, California.*

Right: *An H Bar C square dance counter card, 1960s–70s. Features a matching shirt and dress set. Courtesy of Dan Shapiro, Southwest, Ltd., Costa Mesa, California.*

"Swing Your Partner"

Margaret and Frank ("Guido" before emigrating to the United States) Miele were embroidery contractors for H Bar C from 1947 until the company closed in 1999, according to Dan Shapiro, operator of Southwest, Ltd., in Costa Mesa, California, a company that trades in new/old vintage Western merchandise. They did a lot of the design themselves. Margaret had worked in sportswear for many years before going into Western. Frank was instrumental in design. Margaret handled the actual embroidery, at first doing it herself, and later, training other staff in order to increase production. She was an artist and did hand-machined work. Dan says she referred to it as "chain stitch" embroidery. (However, in this book we distinguish between chain stitching that has light coverage and thin yarn versus chenille, which is also chain stitched but with heavy yarns and high coverage.) They drew the design, then did a punch-hole pattern, which was drawn onto the fabric with chalk. Each part of the shirt was embroidered in pieces and later sewn together.

The fact that we know Margaret and Frank's work is a holdover from earlier times when Western tailors made custom shirts one by one. The names of the craftspeople in factory environments are typically forgotten over time but not in this case, given their long-term involvement. Also, it must be noted that they were responsible for the more ornate designs, not the automated, computerized common versions, which were contracted elsewhere.

The H Bar C special treatments include two-tones with highly stylized smile pockets, jewels, and rhinestones combined with embroidery, fringe with embroidery and without, and extremely contoured yoke treatments.

H Bar C is famous for its many special makes including embroidery, appliqué, and special design treatments. They were never afraid to take the design to its extreme. Many of these shirts are featured in chapter 3.

Their embroideries are highly collectible and cover the widest range of any brand. They include some of the best examples of chenille and appliqué. The most valuable are early ones with heavy coverage on collar, front and back, cuffs and sleeves. Designs include many florals on two-tones and solids, playing-card motifs, and sunbursts. They also did bonnaz embroidery.

Ironically, H Bar C always used the least expensive serged hem to finish the tail (turned hems never ravel and are only slightly more expensive). Given their expensive special treatments, it is strange that they did not do a premium tail hem.

Also, rising labor costs by the 1970s caused H Bar C to switch to 100 percent polyester from higher-cost fabrics such wool, rayon, and cotton gabardines. The all-poly fabric became dated by the 1980s. It had gained a cheap reputation but they continued to use it for twenty years. This negatively affected opinions of all but the most devoted followers.

H Bar C is known for naming its shirt designs. Marvin Parsons, a retailer from Wyoming who later worked for H Bar C, and now for Rockmount, recalls that shirts were named after places by dropping straight pins above an atlas. Naming shirts seems quaint in the age where computers require inventory stock items to be numbered.

Many styles ran indefinitely, making it difficult to date them. Small details changed over time, the result of changes in manufacturing and trends, such as labels, fabric content, and collar lengths. H Bar C held a strong brand presence from the late 1940s through the Urban Cowboy of the late '70s, over thirty years. However, when the Urban Cowboy ended, so did the first time Western wear had gone mass market. Many Western companies closed. While H Bar C survived, it began an eighteen-year-long decline.

Bernie passed away in 1978, leaving Seymour to run the company alone until his death in 1996. At that time company ownership left the Christenfeld family. The company never recovered and finally closed in 1999, after one hundred and two years. How many companies make it half this long? Family businesses characterize much of the Western industry and transition is perhaps their greatest challenge. When you consider the hard work of so many that goes into building a business that lasts for generations, it is sad to see one end.

Much of this information comes from Dan Shapiro, operator of Southwest, Ltd., in Costa Mesa, California, a company that trades in new/old vintage Western merchandise. Dan spent years getting to know Seymour and the H Bar C story. He is perhaps the single best authority on the company and has seen more of it over the years than just about anyone. A devotee to H Bar C, he has a broader collection of H Bar C vintage shirts, advertising, and memorabilia than anyone else. Most of H Bar C's archival material was lost in the sale and closure of the company, so Dan's is the best-known collection.

Unlike most manufacturers who discount goods as they age to maintain cash flow, H Bar C had the luxury of not having to turn its inventory, and H Bar C became known for accumulating old merchandise. Seymour figured that since old goods do not eat anything, why let them go for cheap? Over time, he filled whole warehouses full of old merchandise, time capsules to be picked over by cognoscenti collectors. Eventually, however, the remaining inventory was sold bulk to liquidators.

H Bar C was one of the key companies that helped popularize Western wear. Many people and families devoted their lives to its success. It played a key part in establishing the look that won the hearts and minds of thousands around the world. Some might say it's the natural selection of the market at work when a business closes. It's also the loss of a little piece of all of us.

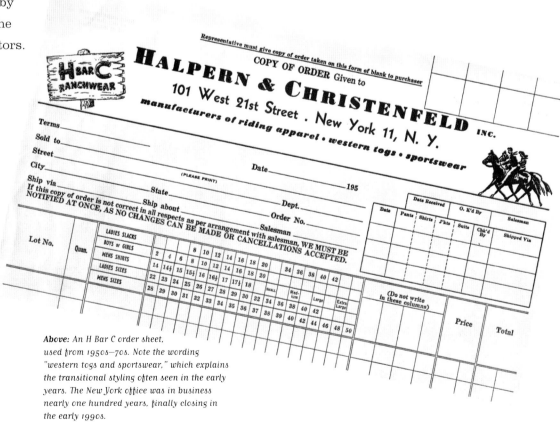

Above: An H Bar C order sheet, used from 1950s–70s. Note the wording "western togs and sportswear," which explains the transitional styling often seen in the early years. The New York office was in business nearly one hundred years, finally closing in the early 1990s.

Another large corrugated mural H Bar C had created for retail stores from 1960—70s. Courtesy of Dan Shapiro, Southwest, Ltd., Costa Mesa, California.

For Collectors of H Bar C ★

Label Dating Guide

H Bar C and California Ranchwear had a huge number of labels over the years. It is especially difficult to date H Bar C by style because of the length of time that styles were produced, so the labels are important in that effort.

—Upper and lower casing is how text appears on the actual label.

—Brown "H BAR C CALIFORNIA RANCHWEAR" in lariat on white: 1940s.

—Brown "H BAR C RANCHWEAR CALIFORNIA," rider on horse, mountains, and cactus on tan: 1940s.

—Brown script "Tailored by CALIFORNIA RANCHWEAR Los Angeles": 1940s–50s.

—Brown "H BAR C" in wood sign, green "CALIFORNIA RANCHWEAR": 1950s.

—V-shaped red taped label "H BAR C, California ranchwear women's": 1960s–70s.

—Black "H BAR C" in less-defined lariat than the 1940s' version, "MADE IN USA," with printed size tag: 1980s.

—Orange "High Sierra," red "H Bar C" on black: 1980s.

—Black "AUTHENTIC WESTERN WEAR" in lariat on white: 1980s.

—Blue script "H BAR C," red "DESIGNER COLLECTION": 1980s.

★ ★

CHAPTER 7

★ ★ ★ ★ ★ ★ ★

LEVI STRAUSS

& Co.

Apparel was in Levi Strauss' genes. Born in Bavaria in 1829, Levi Strauss was the son of a German dry-goods peddler. He immigrated to New York City in 1847 where he worked in his brothers' dry goods business. By 1853, he had gold fever and moved to San Francisco to establish a business under his own name and to represent his brothers' New York firm. Strauss' goldmine proved to be supplying the miners who bought his goods.

His brother-in-law, David Stern, joined him early on and together they built a dry goods business selling everything from fabric to corsets and undergarments. Their customers were tailors, peddlers, and merchants in the Western states.

In 1872, a tailor named Jacob Davis from Reno, Nevada, enlisted Strauss as a partner to patent his idea to rivet the pocket corners on work trousers. With the granting of the patent on May 20, 1873, the pair began to manufacture their "patent riveted overalls" out of denim and created what evolved into blue jeans, the single most iconic style of American clothing other than Western shirts, which Levi Strauss & Co. (LS&CO) also made over the years.

The dry goods company expanded into apparel manufacturing in 1873 and Jacob Davis headed this side of the business. When Levi Strauss died in 1902, his stock went largely to his nephews, David Stern's sons. Control of the company has remained in the family ever since.

LS&CO has the deepest roots of any manufacturer of Western shirts. Perhaps the oldest continuing apparel label in the United States and the most famous brand in the world, LS&CO has had a fundamental role in the overall apparel business. It was in business fifty years ahead of H Bar C's predecessor, the second-oldest Western apparel brand, now defunct. While Western shirts did not emerge until the 1930s, LS&CO was deeply entrenched in the emerging Western lifestyle long before lifestyle was even a concept. Famous for inventing jeans, LS&CO also was a significant early force in Western apparel, though it did not continuously pursue that direction.

Above: An in-store advertising piece for Levi's™ Western shirts, run in the early 1950s. Courtesy of Levi Strauss & Co. Archives, San Francisco, California.

LS&CO expanded into work shirts in the late 1800s, according to Lynn Downey, company Historian. The earliest known LS&CO shirt label is the Sunset label. The details of the earliest shirts were lost in the 1906 earthquake and fire. In the early 1920s, LS&CO made denim work shirts that cowboys wore with jeans. These early shirts bear no resemblance to what would become classic Western style. They were loose and plain, designed to be worn with the work overalls. The cowboy link with LS&CO products and marketing appeared in the company's promotional materials by 1899. The book *This Is a Pair of Levi's Jeans* (published by Levi Strauss & Co.) documents some of the early cowboy-theme ads. Several "trade cards" feature cowboys. A circa 1905 catalog cover with a Frederick Remington–like illustration of two cowboys roping has the headline, "All Over the West They Wear Levi Strauss & Co.'s Copper Riveted Overall."

WESTERN WEAR
CATALOGUE
SPRING 1959

Prepared for C. R. ANTHONY COMPANY

LEVI'S
AMERICA'S FINEST
OVERALL
SINCE 1850

Above: The cover of the Levi's Western Wear retailer catalog, Spring 1959. Courtesy of Levi Strauss & Co. Archives, San Francisco, California.

LS&CO was well aware of its popularity with cowboys by the 1930s. Downey states that Walter Haas Sr., a descendent of David Stern and grandfather of the current chairman of the board, Bob Haas, selected the cowboy to become the brand's icon. Cowboys had worn LS&CO products for years and the company capitalized on that loyalty in its marketing. The rising popularity of dude ranches in the West contributed to this direction at LS&CO. Visitors from the East took home what they purchased and wore while out West.

During the Depression, workingmen continued to be LS&CO's primary market. Around 1938, LS&CO launched a sportswear line with Western flavoring called Dude Ranch Duds. The line included denim jeans and jackets, gabardine pants and shirts, and satin shirts.

These early, transitional Western shirts featured offset flap pockets and smile pockets, shank and sew-through buttons, straight back yokes (but no front yokes), and came in a wide range of colors. Some had contrasting piping and others had horse or steer embroidery—both early Western design elements. The fancier shirts themselves were labeled rodeo shirts, as opposed to the simple work shirts.

Perhaps the reason LS&CO is one of the most enduring brands in the world is because it has never been afraid to reinvent itself. According to the LS&CO Web site, in the 1940s the company "made the tough decision to shift from dry goods wholesaling, which represented the majority of our business at the time, and to focus instead on making and selling jeans, jean jackets, shirts and Western wear. It was a foresighted—though risky—decision that enabled us to develop and prosper."

The LS&CO archive has no catalogs from the 1940s to the late 1950s to precisely date shirts during that period. The first snap shirts appear in the 1959 catalog. At that time there was a wide range of fabrics and pocket styles. Snap shirts were produced until the late 1970s. The demise of the Urban Cowboy fad seems to have prompted LS&CO to consciously leave the Western business after being a mainstay for over forty years. The company stopped sponsoring rodeos and dropped the Western theme from its advertising. According to Downey, "the link with the West" was dropped because "it didn't really reflect our brand as much."

Dropping Western was just one of many major moves the company has undertaken in recent years. Also significant was its decision to sell to the big, chain discount stores. Garment production was shifted overseas and its last U.S. factory was closed as it approached 150 years in business.

It is especially interesting that LS&CO's link to the iconic cowboy helped transform the brand into an icon itself. It was an alternative fashion for working men and, later, cowboys, long before alternative was cool. Later, in the 1950s and '60s, it was a hip protest statement to conventional fashion. Ironically it became mainstream, appealing to most everyone from all walks of life. The LS&CO Web site says, "Generations of people have worn our products as a symbol of freedom and self-expression in the face of adversity, challenge and social change. They forged a new territory called the American West. They fought in wars for peace. They instigated counterculture revolutions. They tore down the Berlin Wall. Reverent, irreverent—they all took a stand."

LEVI STRAUSS MAKERS OF AUTHENTIC

7068
ROYAL BLUE

6092
RODEO SHIRT

2680
BOYS' PLAID

2020
MEN'S PLAID

7027 — MEN'S BLACK PIPED IN WHITE
7028 — MEN'S WHITE PIPED IN BLACK
Made exactly as 7082
SIZES: 14 to 17. Pkd. 3/12 solid.

6092—LADIES' MAN-STYLE RODEO SHIRT
A dressy shirt of satin finished rayon. A shirt
with true WESTERN GLAMOUR, style and
detail for the Gal who wants real Western
shirts "like the Wranglers wear."
SIZES: 30 to 40. Pkd. 3/12 Ass't.
COLORS: Maroon, Blue, Gold.
Each shirt with contrasting color piping.

2685 — BOYS' COWBOY MOTIF SHIRT
A washable Western figured boys' shirt, made
to tub, that can really "stand the gaff.'
SIZES: 6 to 14½. Pkd. 3/12.
COLORS: Varied assortment.

2020 — MEN'S PLAID SHIRTS
Vivid colorings make this a popular assortment. A closely woven, fast-color fabric, with
hard wearing qualities.
SIZES: 14 to 17. Pkd. 3/12 Ass't.

7068 — MEN'S ROYAL BLUE SHIRTS

Has real "Way Out West" appeal. This highly
lustrous, Panne Satin Western Rodeo shirt, of
American loomed Rayon, is made with beauti-
fully embroidered Long-Horn Steer-Heads on
pockets Has Western diagonal cuffs.

SIZES: 14 to 17. Pkd. 3/12 Ass't.
COLORS: Blue, Maroon, Gold.

**7082 — MEN'S GOLD COLOR WITH
BLACK PIPING**
Like a WESTERN SUNSET! A fine tough

2680 — BOYS' PLAID COWBOY SHIRTS

WESTERN RIDING WEAR SINCE 1850

7041
MEN'S BLACK

6182
LADIES' PLAID

7052
HORSE AND
STEER MODEL

6178
BLUE WITH
WHITE PIPING

7074 — MEN'S SHIRT, RUST COLOR, PIPED IN WHITE

As soft as the after glow of a Western sunset is this new velvety-feel satin shirt. A Cow-punchers shirt that is also durable. With rounded flaps on pockets, and finely tailored diagonal three button cuffs, contrasting pearl buttons and piped neatly throughout.

SIZES: 14 to 17. Pkd. 1/12.

COLORS:

7074—Rust, Piped in White	7077—Gold, Piped in Black
7075—White, Piped in Black	7078—Blue, Piped in White
7076—Black, Piped in White	7079—Maroon, Piped in White

6178—LADIES' MAN-STYLE MODELS

Exactly as 7074

SIZES: 30 to 40. Pkd. 1/12.

COLORS:

6174—Rust, Piped in White	6177—Gold, Piped in Black.
6175—White, Piped in Black	6178—Blue, Piped in White
6176—Black, Piped in White	6179—Maroon, Piped in White

6182 — LADIES' PLAID SHIRTS, MAN-STYLE

These Seersuckers need no ironing—just wash and . . . "That's All". A proven cloth for the

2682 — BOYS' PLAID SHIRTS

Models and fabrics exactly as No. 6182
SIZES: 6 to 14½. Pkd. 3/12 Ass't.

6183 — LADIES' PLAID SHIRTS, MAN-STYLE

Construction as 6182.

Made in gingham plaids that are a brilliant blend of high colorings. Washable and color-fast.

SIZES: 30 to 40. Pkd. 3/12 Ass't.

7041—MEN'S BLACK SATIN SHIRTS

These lustrous colorings ride high, wide and handsome with Westerners. Made from heavy American loomed satin rayon, the large, piped, half moon, arrow pockets set this garment off

7052 — MEN'S SHIRTS, HORSE AND STEER MODEL

This is a BEST SELLER. Made from durable satin-finished heavy rayon. Has finely em-broidered horse and steer heads at base of each half moon pocket.

SIZES: 14 to 17. Pkd. 1/12.

COLORS:

7050—White, Piped in Black	7053—Blue, Piped in White
7051—Black, Piped in White	7054—Maroon, Piped in White
7052—Gold, Piped in Black	7059—Rust, Piped in White

LADIES' MAN-STYLE SHIRTS, HORSE AND STEER MODEL

For Collectors of Levi ★★★★★★★★★★★★★★★★★★★★★★★★

Levi Strauss & Co. is one of the oldest apparel manufacturers in the world. As the originator of jeans, this brand had an immense impact on fashion over its 150-year history. Early Levi's-branded products and advertising memorabilia bring some of the highest prices of apparel-related collectibles. While Levi's jeans command astronomical prices, particularly in Japan, its shirts are very collectible too.

Label Dating Guide

The earliest Levi's work shirts date from the late 1800s, but Western style shirts did not emerge until the 1930s. Highly stylized Western shirts date to the 1950s and '60s. Production stopped in the late 1970s. Upper and lower casing is how text appears on the actual label.

—Sunset brand shirts: late 1890s.

—Two-tone brown on off-white with large steer skull, "LEVI STRAUSS, MAKERS OF LEVI'S OVERALLS AUTHENTIC, AUTHENTIC WESTERN WEAR" (in jagged edge sign), "Dryclean only," with second color beige horizontal lines: 1940s.

—Black on off-white horse rider, black block letters "Levi Strauss," lariat style "Rodeo Shirt": 1930s–40s.

—Two-tone brown and red on off-white with small steer skull, red "Levi's" reversed, brown jagged edge sign with "AUTHENTIC WESTERN WEAR," red "LEVI STRAUSS OF CALIFORNIA": 1950s–60s.

—Two-tone blue and red on white with cowboy holding branding LS iron and saddle, red "Levi's" reversed, blue "AUTHENTIC," red "WESTERN WEAR", blue "LEVI STRAUSS & CO, SAN FRANCISCO": 1960s.

★★★★★★★★★★★★★★★★★★★★★★★★★★★★★★★★★★★★

TODOS USAN
Los Pantalones Overalls con Remaches de Cobre, de
LEVI STRAUSS

HE AQUÍ ALGUNOS DE LOS RECORDS DEL AÑO 1926, QUE NOS ENORGULLECEN:

❡ Glenn Hibbs, Golconda, Nevada, **Ganó el Primer Premio en el Concurso de Atar Caballos Cerriles de Winnemucca, Nevada, Rodeo,** del 4, 5 y 6 de Septiembre de 1926, usando durante el concurso nuestros Overalls.

❡ Bud Arnold, de Elgin, Oregon, **Campeon del Concurso de Jineteo del Union County Fair, Elgin, Oregon,** del 22 al 25 de Septiembre de 1926, usando durante todo el concurso Overalls Levi Strauss, Marca Piel de Gamuza; todos los demas participantes los usaron tambien.

❡ Perry Ivory, **Victorioso en el Concurso de Mejor Vaquero, en el Rodeo del Valle de San Joaquin,** el 4, 5, 6 y 7, de Septiembre de 1926, usó Overalls de Levi durante los cuatro dias del concurso, y dice que son los únicos que usa.

Lawton Champie en su traje de trabajo para todos los dias— Overalls y **Chaqueta** de LEVI STRAUSS

De gran servicio para hombres y muchachos que trabajan duro y cuya ropa se sujeta a mucho uso.

En el **Concurso de Cheyenne, Wyoming, Frontier Days,** que se verificó del 27 de Julio de 1926 al 31 de Julio de 1926:

En las **Carreras de Caballos Corridas** cada dia del concurso, todas con caballos cerriles salieron victoriosos:

El 27 de Julio, Yakima Kid;

El 28 de Julio, Bud Clark;

El 29 de Julio, Floud Stillings;

El 30 de Julio, H. W. Collin;

El 31 de Julio, Albert Christenson.

Cada uno de los vencedores usó los Overalls de Levi, lo cual consta de la siguiente certificación:

"A QUIEN ESTE INTERESADO:

Uno de los resultados mas extraordinarios de las fiestas recientes que se verificaron en Cheyenne, fue que cada uno de los participantes que ganaron primer premio usan Overalls de Levi Strauss, Marca Dos Caballos. No hay duda que son los mejores Overalls para jinetes.

[FIRMA] WM. G. HAAS,
Director a Cargo de las Fiestas Cheyenne Frontier Days, 1926."

RECUERDE —La Siguiente Garantia se Encuentra en Cada Par de LEVI'S:

Un Par Nuevo GRATIS si se Descosen

LEVI STRAUSS & CO.
SAN FRANCISCO, CAL.
COPPER RIVETED
QUALITY CLOTHING. XX
TRADE MARK
PATENTED MAY 20 1873
Every Garment Guaranteed
Lot W L

Facsimile de la Marca Piel de Gamuza, No. 1 XX

SIZE LEVI STRAUSS & CO.
SAN FRANCISCO, CAL.
COPPER RIVETED
CLOTHING.
LOT TRADE MARK
PATENTED MAY 20 1873
Every Garment Guaranteed

Facsimile de la Marca de Genero, No. 2

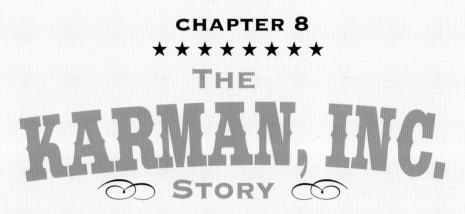

CHAPTER 8

THE KARMAN, INC. STORY

Karman, Inc., is an early member of the "Denver School of Western Apparel." Karman's founder, Sam Mandelbaum, was twenty years old when he began working at Miller & Co. in 1935. He would later return to work there after World War II.

The son of a tailor, young Sam had no particular interest in pursuing that side of the business, but he would prove to possess a canny flair for manufacturing and marketing shirts for ranchers, cowboys, and farmers. After graduating from high school, Sam found work in a wholesale food market in Denver's lower downtown warehouse area (now the historic residential and entertainment district called LoDo). This job was barely a step above unemployment in those days when the country was in the grips of the Depression. While money and jobs were scarce, young Sam made a move up to Miller & Co., the thriving wholesale and retail Western apparel business that gave many a start in the business.

The company manufactured and distributed apparel to chain stores, mercantile, and menswear stores in the Western United States. Sam worked in the wholesale division until the United States entered World War II. By 1942, he was married and had a one-year-old daughter, but Sam soon found himself in France where he rose to the rank of master sergeant. He served in the army until Germany surrendered in 1945.

Back from the war, Sam returned to Miller & Co. where he resumed working in the wholesale division. "Sam's job was to coordinate things at the factory—deciding on fabrics, scheduling deliveries, that sort of thing," recalls his son, Gary Mandelbaum. Sam eventually became involved in the design.

"Design back then was very different than what you would call design work today," Gary says. "Styles didn't change; there wasn't a lot of innovation. The economy back then was just getting started after the war. They worked in an economy where there were a lot of shortages; they were lucky to get stuff. It wasn't the mass consumerism that we know today. There wasn't much demand for fashion then, especially in rural America."

Left: A Karman wholesale catalog cover, 1956. Courtesy of Karman, Denver, Colorado.

KARMAN
INCORPORATED
Western Wear

1513 WAZEE   DENVER, COLORADO

MATCHING FAMILY WESTERN SET

DAN RIVER GINGHAM PLAID   •   LITTLE OR NO IRONING FINISH

Rich woven ombre plaid with sparkling gold mylar stripe. Matching fabric and colors for the entire family. Authentic Western form-fit yoke model. Diamond shaped pearlized snaps.
COLORS: Blue, Green, Brown Asstd. to box.

- Mens' No. 1545   Dozen..$45.00 Pack 3/12
- Ladies' No. 1345   Dozen..$30.00 Pack 3/12
- Boys' No. 1445   Dozen..$30.00 Pack 4/12
- Girls' No. 1645   Dozen..$22.50 Pack 4/12

advertised in LIFE
Wrinkl-Shed
with Dri-Don
the ultimate in carefree wash and wear cottons
an exclusive fabric development
by DAN RIVER®
Fabrics with fashion woven in!

1958

Spring and Summer Catalog

TERMS: 2% 20 DAYS—NET 30 • F. O. B. DENVER
ALL PRICES SUBJECT TO CHANGE WITHOUT NOTICE

Above: *Karman Western Wear wholesale catalog back cover, 1958. The wholesale price for men's plaid shirts was $45 per dozen. Courtesy of Karman, Denver, Colorado.*

With its emphasis on producing work clothes for farmers and ranchers, the design and manufacturing emphasis was more on function and durability than on style. Sam worked at Miller until 1948, when he had a falling out with his boss, Jack A. Weil, a company principal. Gary says, "They agreed to disagree and Sam left."

Sam saw opportunity in the nascent Western business. He had his own ideas about making and selling shirts. Sam set out to start his own company and found a backer in Jack Karsh, a local investor. The new company was named for the first three letters of Karsh and Mandelbaum; Karman, Inc. opened for business in October, 1948. Sam stayed in LoDo, but this time as his own boss. Karsh was a silent partner.

The young company concentrated on shirts for ranchers, farmers, and cowhands. The first line included ten pieces with fundamental Western shirt styling: pointed front and back yokes, two front flap pockets, and snaps instead of buttons. Karman was a small shop with two or three employees. "When it was getting off the ground, Sam went on the road selling it," Gary Mandelbaum says of the early days. "He'd come back with the orders, try to get it produced, and have a few people ship it."

In 1949, Sam brought his brother-in-law into the company as an active partner. His father-in-law invested some money to get his son, Leonard Silverberg, into the business. Sam was president and Leonard, vice president. Sam designed the shirts and oversaw production, sales, and distribution. Leonard took care of the back office duties and cash flow. The pair worked as a team. "Every function Sam and he would do together," Gary says. Karsh was bought out in the early '50s.

By 1950 Karman's shirt business had grown enough to hire its first sales representative, John McIllece. "Sam was covering the territory; Leonard was running the office," Gary Mandelbaum says. By turning the established territory over to a salesman, Sam was able to spread out and develop new territories. The business—and the company's sales force—grew in a distinct pattern. "Sam would start to build a territory, then get a salesperson to take over," Gary says.

John traveled Colorado, Wyoming, and Montana. "John was our first salesman and he was with us until the late '70s," Gary recalls. "His son, Rich McIllece, then took over the territory. John was our number-one salesman back then and Rich is our number-one salesman now."

In the early days, Karman's shirt production was ten to fifteen dozen shirts per week, according to Gary. The shirts were priced about the same as other basic Western shirts in the '40s: the going wholesale price was $12.50–$24 per dozen. "If a shirt was $24 a dozen, that means it was $2 apiece, so it was $3.99 retail," Gary says. Embroidery and other decorative flourishes increased the price. By the late '50s, Western shirts were getting higher prices as their costs and perceived value went up. The company was putting out forty-five dozen shirts a week in 1957, at an average wholesale price of $48 per dozen.

Below: Karman wholesale catalog page, 1960s. Features young Gary Mandelbaum in the center of bottom-left photo. Courtesy of Karman, Denver, Colorado.

"My dad made friends with people from a factory that made for Miller," Gary says. "He went to those factories and they started to make shirts for him. They were made in Pennsylvania and in Arkansas. By 1952, Sam had enough production to go to a friend in Mississippi, Rex Brown at Itawamba Manufacturing. Eventually we bought the company in the 1980s."

Basic styles changed little in the '50s; changes were made in patterns, colors, or fabrics. "You changed colors to give the customer a reason to buy," Gary explains. "It was different from what they already had. If you bought it this spring, you didn't want to see it [again] next spring."

Shirt designing at Karman was done by management and sales reps until 1981 when the first designer was hired. "Up until then, people who worked in the company designed the garments," he says. "My dad thought he was a designer."

Gary says the notion of designing was completely different then. "It's not like today where you have to have a design team designing the pattern and the coloration," he explains. "I helped design shirts from '71 to '80, and that's when I said, 'Whoa, we need some new lines.'"

Over the years, Karman has marketed numerous brand names and lines with different labels. In 1956, Sam purchased Tem-Tex, a small Texas apparel company. It is not clear whether he acquired the whole company or if he just bought the name. The Tem-Tex brand became a second shirt line, dressier than Karman.

Karman began to expand its dressier and fancier shirt offerings and expanded its market. Influences like the television show *Davy Crockett,* and Western movies influenced their shirt design during the 1950s. Among the novelty designs in company catalogs are fringed and lace-up

Feldt Mfg., located in Stamford, Texas, produced Tem-Tex. Gary Mandelbaum says the name is derived from the town of Temple, Texas. Under Feldt, during the 1950s, Tem-Tex made some extremely stylized designs. These pieces made in Texas have special treatments that make them very collectible. See chapter 3 for examples of their highly detailed yokes, pockets, and cuffs.

pullovers. Gary says the fanciest of these shirts appealed mostly to urban dwellers.

By the late '50s they started to introduce ladies' apparel. The earliest ladies' styles matched the men's and boys' shirts. The "matching shirts" were a hit with the family-oriented culture of the 1950s.

Karman also began trying new fabrics as they came on the market. Polyester became the hot ticket in a culture that was snapping up time- and labor-saving home appliances. Even as consumers bought more sophisticated irons, they bought shirts that required little or no ironing. No little irony in that.

The precursor to permanent-press polyester was resin-baked cotton. "You would take a finished garment, put it on a hanger, and it had a certain resin already incorporated in the fiber," Gary says. "You would put it into heat in an actual walk-in oven—we used to put racks of shirts in them—and bake them . . . . It gave the shirt memory so it would not wrinkle. It was one hell of a hard product." In the late '50s, baking was replaced by polyester.

With revolutionary new fabrics, Karman further expanded its styling and color offerings and experimented with new and unusual patterns. Floral prints in

By the late 1950s Karman started to introduce ladies' apparel. The earliest ladies' styles matched the men's and boys' shirts. The "matching shirts" were a hit with the family-oriented culture of the 1950s.

the late '60s and early '70s were masculine colorations of ladies' floral prints, Gary notes. "It was a look that was never seen before—or since," he concedes.

Gary grew up in his dad's business. He even modeled boys' shirts for their catalogs. After studying business and marketing in college, he joined the company full-time in 1971. He took over Karman in the late '80s and later became president.

Innovations from the line ramped up in 1981 with the arrival of shirt designer Nancy Leavitt. One of her inspirations was the Western border print. "In the late '70s, converters in New

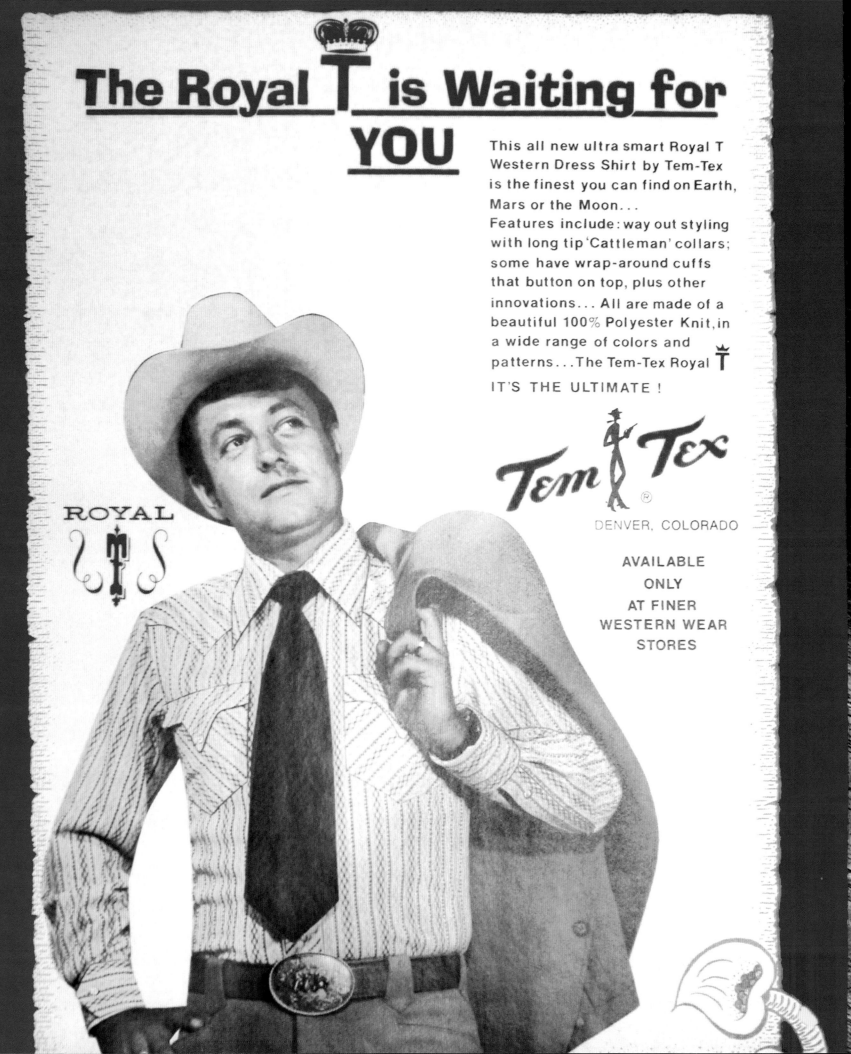

Above: Gary Mandelbaum, Kenny Rogers, and Sam Mandelbaum, 1980s. Courtesy of Karman, Denver, Colorado.

York were making floral dress border prints, and we engineered them into border shirts," Gary recalls. "Nancy took it to the next level and created Aztec borders, and then she was the first one to create theme borders. It's really due to her artistic, creative talent that she brought that whole look to the Western market. For years everyone tried to copy it, but they couldn't come close."

Another bold step for Karman was hooking up with country singer Kenny Rogers to license the Kenny Rogers Collection, which debuted shortly after the end of the Urban Cowboy boom.

Karman's place in the history of Western apparel was secured with its smart marketing and sensitivity to consumers' needs and tastes. It survived the aftermath of the Urban Cowboy era by focusing on design and paying attention to market changes. The company sold its prime LoDo property in the late '90s and moved to modern offices in suburban Denver with warehouse facilities nearby. About this time, the company shifted its name from Karman to Roper, one of its brands. Western shirt production was also shifted offshore.

Left: A Tem-Tex Royal T magazine color ad, 1960–70s. Courtesy of Karman, Denver, Colorado.

For Collectors of Karman and Tem-Tex Shirts ★ ★ ★

Karman, a major manufacturer of Western wear, is Denver-based. They made many brands including Karman, Round-up, Tem-Tex, Hi-Rider, Roper, the Kenny Rogers Western Collection, and Looney Tunes Western Collection.

These vintage brands are not known for special treatments; the basic designs are seen most often on the vintage-shirt market. Karman's emphasis was more towards fine basic design and not about the more flamboyant features that command higher prices. The Karman label represents a broad range of fabrics and colors. Tem-Tex, particularly in the early years, represents highly detailed makes.

Label Dating Guide

—"Form-fitted Karman Western shirts, Denver, Colorado" on sign hanging from rough-hewn logs: 1950s–60s.

—"Roper" spelled in green rope script, cowboy, saguaro cactus and mountains, off-white background: 1950s.

—"Tem-Tex" in brown on tan, "Made in the Heart of Texas" inside a lariat loop, cowboy lower-left corner: pre-Karman, made before 1957 by Feldt Manufacturing.

—"Tem-Tex" in red on tan, "Oven baked permanent press, Western sportswear," size stamped on collar: made by Karman, late 1950s.

—"Round-up" in rope script, rider with lariat, mountains: 1960s.

—"Karman" in red letters, white Buffalo head, brown background: 1970s.

—"Gold Collection," on white, "Karman" in gold on black: 1970s–80s.

—"Silver Collection" in black letters on silver, "Karman" in silver on black: 1970s–80s.

—Red "Tem-Tex" with cowboy in center in black, "Western Flair Sportswear": 1970s.

—Red "temtex" on black, glued label: 1980s.

—Black "Tem-Tex" on gold on black, sewn on sides only: 1970s–80s.

—"Kenny Rogers Western Collection (gold letters) by Karman (white letters)," silhouette on brown: 1980s.

—"Kenny Rogers WESTERN COLLECTION by Karman" red lettering on white background: 1980s.

—"Looney Tunes Western Collection by Karman": 1990s.

★ ★

Facing: A Tem-Tex magazine ad, 1971. Features rodeo, movie and music stars. Karman began using celebrity endorsements in the 1960s and continued to use them through the '90s. Also shown is a black-and-white wholesale catalog page, 1960s. Courtesy of Karman, Denver, Colorado.

GET WITH THE
TEM-TEX PERSONALITY PARADE

CHUCK PARKISON
Rodeo Announcer

BILL HOLT
Rodeo Announcer

IVAN DAINES
Rodeo Champ

SLIM PICKENS
Movies and TV

REX ALLEN
"Mr. Cowboy"

Hat by
Eddy Bros.

HANK THOMPSON and the BRAZOS VALLEY BOYS - ALL IN TEM-TEX WESTERNS

Tem Tex ®

DENVER, COLO.

**STEP OUT IN TEM-TEX
WESTERN FLAIR SPORTSWEAR
At Finer Western Stores Everywhere**

LANA BRACKENBURY
MISS RODEO AMERICA 1971

92

CHAPTER 9
★★★★★★★★★★

∽ THE ∽

WESTMOOR STORY

While Denver was the fountainhead for early Western shirt manufacturers, several companies were based elsewhere. Westmoor, maker of the popular Panhandle Slim line of Western shirts, got its start in an unlikely location: Minneapolis.

Brothers Martin and Ernest Hochster immigrated to the United States from Germany in the 1930s and settled in New York City. Ernest worked as assistant production manager for Excello, a men's shirt company. Martin sold ladies' apparel. They both moved to Minnesota in 1946, where Ernest put together a group of partners to produce men's shirts in Minneapolis. He named the company Westmoor, Inc., to reflect the company's interest in making shirts for farmers and ranchers, according to Jeff Hochster, Ernest's oldest son and successor as president. Jeff adds that "moor" was a popular ending for company names in the late 1940s.

Minneapolis and its sister-city, St. Paul, were bustling metropolitan cities sitting astride the Mississippi River at its convergence with two other rivers, the St. Croix and the Minnesota. This is the northernmost stretch of the Mississippi navigable for barges and other cargo-bearing river vessels. The Twin Cities were important milling centers for Midwest grain, as well as for lumber logged from the vast hardwood forests of northern Minnesota and Wisconsin. The area was heavily populated with German immigrant farmers and their descendants. Its manufacturing base and Germanic population seemed to the Hochsters like a good place to start an apparel company.

Everything was under one roof—production, packaging, marketing, sales, and warehousing. The focus was on casual apparel, especially the relatively new category of sports shirts. Ernest designed most of the shirts, according to Jeff. "They were playing a little bit with the Western lifestyle at that time," Jeff says, but the bulk of the Westmoor line was mainstream, conventional styling for rural customers. Different lines had different names, such as Westmoor Sportswear and House of Westmoor.

Right: *Ernest Hochester (far right) selling in the showroom, 1950s. Courtesy of Westmoor, Fort Worth, Texas.*

Above: A Panhandle Slim black-and-white catalog sheet featuring a shirt with a very contoured one-piece yoke/pocket flap treatment. 1950–60s. Courtesy of Westmoor, Fort Worth, Texas.

Right: A Panhandle Slim black-and-white magazine ad, 1970s. Courtesy of Westmoor, Fort Worth, Texas.

The finest Western Shirts have this label

No other maker of Western Shirts uses the same quality control, or has a wider selection of miracle and absolute permanent-press fabrics. No other makes shirts with longer tails or in more styles. For over 20 years the number one quality Western Shirt maker. Only in price do we cut corners. Retails from $6.95.

In 1948 or '49, Westmoor began putting snaps on some of their shirts at the behest of customers. Westmoor's first Western shirt was called "The Gambler."

"That was the first real Western shirt that we did," Jeff says. The Gambler featured a three-button cuff and a long tail. When the shirt sold well in the West and Southwest, Ernest's salesmen convinced him that they could get even more sales if the shirt had a yoke and snaps.

Westmoor's first Western shirts were made of wool or rayon gabardine and came with either snaps or buttons. "We gave them a choice," recalls Ernest, who retired from Westmoor in the mid '90s.

The name Panhandle Slim was the brainchild of Westmoor's first sales representative. "We had a salesman named Ed Gassman who was traveling Texas for us at the time," Jeff says. "He said we needed to have more of a real Western brand name. He was up in Amarillo at the time calling on an account, and my father said to him, 'Do you have any suggestions?' He came up with the idea to conjure up a cowboy with the name. The impression was that Texans were tall and lean, and he was out in the panhandle of Texas and thought it was an interesting name, so he put the two ideas together and came up with Panhandle Slim."

High labor and other costs in Minnesota prompted Ernest to buy out his partners and uproot the company, lock, stock, and barrel in 1954. He moved his company and his young family to Nebraska, where business and living expenses were more accommodating.

"In 1954, my father had been looking for a factory to purchase somewhere outside of Minnesota," Jeff recalls. "He found a factory in Nebraska City, Nebraska. It had been the former Thunderbird shirt factory. He moved our family to Omaha, and he commuted fifty miles every day for the better part of eight years."

Ernest's focus shifted to Western shirts in Nebraska City. He also hired his first designer there. Leola "Ole" Edmonston had been working for Thunderbird when Hochster bought the company and factory. She designed Panhandle Slim shirts from 1954 until her retirement in the late '60s.

Tired of the fifty-mile commute, Ernest sold the Nebraska City factory to Pendleton Woolen Mills in 1962 and started making shirts in Omaha. He also started farming out production to other shirt makers. "At that time we had the factory in Omaha, but we ended up contracting most of our production to factories in the Southeast," Jeff recalls.

"We grew a lot during that period," Jeff continues. He credits his uncle, Martin, with a lot of that growth. Martin had been a silent partner in the business since the beginning. He did not join as an active partner until the early '60s, when he began to develop new sales territories for Westmoor. "Martin had a tendency to move into a territory and travel it," Jeff explains. "Once he opened the territory up, he would hire another salesman to work it."

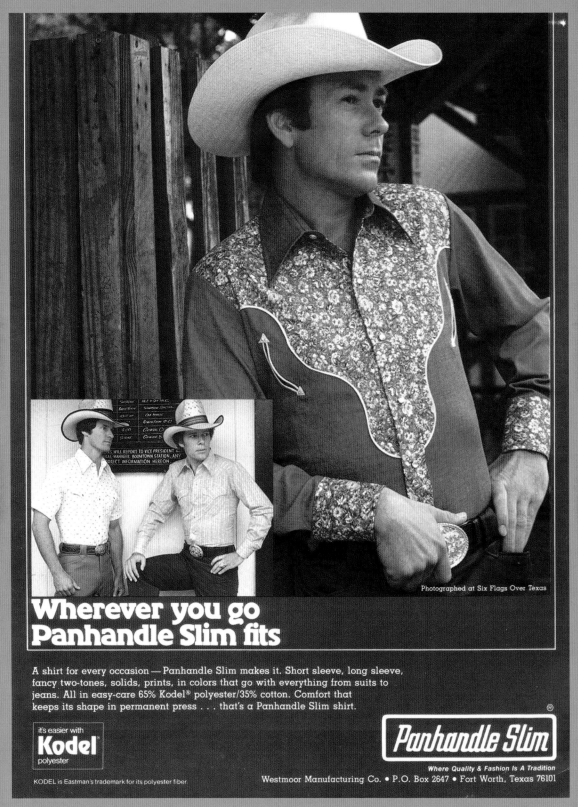

Photographed at Six Flags Over Texas

Wherever you go Panhandle Slim fits

A shirt for every occasion—Panhandle Slim makes it. Short sleeve, long sleeve, fancy two-tones, solids, prints, in colors that go with everything from suits to jeans. All in easy-care 65% Kodel® polyester/35% cotton. Comfort that keeps its shape in permanent press . . . that's a Panhandle Slim shirt.

it's easier with
Kodel
polyester

KODEL is Eastman's trademark for its polyester fiber.

Panhandle Slim ®

Where Quality & Fashion Is A Tradition

Westmoor Manufacturing Co. • P.O. Box 2647 • Fort Worth, Texas 76101

Above: A Panhandle Slim color magazine ad, 1970s. Courtesy of Westmoor, Fort Worth, Texas.

As the oldest son, Jeff also began working for Ernest, sweeping floors and working as a "bundle boy," carrying bundles from one machine operation to the next. He was motivated early on because he wanted to spend time with his dad. "In the '60s when I really could have spent my time doing other things and probably wanted to, my father thought it would be good experience and a good way for me to earn money," Jeff recalls. "It was a humbling experience. I did that in the '60s on weekends and summers."

Jeff studied business in college and went to work for a department-store chain in Nebraska and Kansas as a corporate buyer for two years before returning to Westmoor. At Westmoor, Jeff worked in sales, warehouse management, and merchandising, but says he "pretty much kept the sales responsibility." He became president of Westmoor in the late '80s.

Jeff's younger brother, Lenny, also studied business in college and then worked in production for a mainstream shirt maker in New York for three years. Lenny joined Westmoor in the early '80s and became vice president when Ernest retired.

In July 1974, Jeff moved to Fort Worth to open a branch office. His relocation would prove to be the first step in moving the entire company to Texas a year later. "We were losing our building in downtown Omaha to urban renewal, so we were going to have to relocate," he says. "When it came to site selection, it came down to choosing between Dallas and Fort Worth."

Jeff says there was strategic thinking behind the move, as well. "In Omaha, we felt that we were seeing maybe one customer a month, two a month if we were lucky," he explains. "And we wanted to move where there would be a larger percentage of our customer base. That's why we moved to Texas in September, 1975."

Westmoor acquired a new facility on the edge of Fort Worth and has remained in that site ever since.

The '70s proved to be heady years for Westmoor. Whether it was because of the relocation to Fort Worth, improving design and manufacturing quality, a robust economy, or all three, Westmoor's Panhandle Slim shirt business grew by leaps and bounds.

In addition to Panhandle Slim, Westmoor also launched a line called Ranch & Town in 1960. "The Ranch & Town label was a lower-priced, lower-featured garment," Jeff says. For the most part, Westmoor concentrated on these two shirt lines until they shut down the Ranch and Town line in 1997. Forays into other related markets were relatively short lived. "There was a period in probably the late '60s where we got into the wool sport-shirt business," Jeff says. "We bought out a company in Minneapolis called Game and Lake, and we were selling Game and Lake wool shirts. It was a competitor of Pendleton, really nice wool; some of it was domestic and some of it was import. We probably did that for four or five years."

Right: A Panhandle Slim ad, 1970s. Courtesy of Westmoor, Fort Worth, Texas.

Live the Good Life
...in P.S. Style

Panhandle Slim
WESTMOOR MANUFACTURING COMPANY
OMAHA, NEBR. & FT. WORTH, TEX.

Like most of the other major Western shirt makers, there is little archival evidence about the fabrics used in early Panhandle Slim shirts. As noted, the first Panhandle Slim shirts were made with wool or rayon gabardine. That gave way to lighter fabrics in the '50s and '60s, especially with the rise of so-called "miracle fabrics" containing polyester. According to Jeff, Westmoor sold a lot of 80/20 polyester/cotton blend fabrics in solid colors then. "That fabric was referred to as Super Ultra Vino," he recalls. "It was a real top-count 80 poly/20 cotton fabrication. Permanent press became real hot at the time; we did a big, big job in this cloth called Super Ultra Vino, both in snap and button." It was manufactured by a mill called Klopman.

"We also did a lot of Ultressa," he continues, "100 percent polyester solids and prints. In Texas, if you wore Ultressa, you could pretty well guarantee yourself that during the spring and summer, you'd be sweating something terrible."

Polyester and poly/cotton blends would continue to be the mainstay of the shirt line through the '70s. Solids and plaids dominated until prints caught on in the mid '70s, according to Jeff.

Like other Western shirt manufacturers, Panhandle Slim benefited from the boom in sales driven by the Urban Cowboy fad from 1978 to 1981. One thing the company did not do was hike production and pump shirts into the market through mainstream retailers. Jeff views the fad as a watershed in the history of the industry that may have put a lot of new customers in Western apparel, but ultimately signaled the end of an era for Western shirt manufacturers. The biggest problem, Jeff says, was that a lot of poorly made, badly designed shirts flooded the market. Urban Cowboy customers came away with a negative impression of Western shirts.

"A lot people came into the Western wear business who had no business being in it," Jeff contends. "They really didn't know how to make a shirt. There were a lot of problems with the quality."

He says the core Western apparel industry also contributed to the bust that followed the Urban Cowboy sales boom by cranking up production and failing to understand the nature of the exhilarating mechanical bull ride they were on. Ultimately they were tossed off.

"Westmoor didn't go out and sell chain stores," he explains. "Chain stores were starting to sell a lot of Western. We pretty much stuck with our grassroots customers. Their business exploded, don't get me wrong, but we really didn't want to expand our production capabilities only to see them shrink again. We felt it was a fad, so we stuck to our true customer base and just pretty much left that fad customer alone."

Westmoor is one of the few family-owned Western shirt companies to survive the Urban Cowboy fad and its aftermath. The company continues to be a major force in the Western shirt industry. Most of their production is now imported, one of the last companies to shift production abroad. The gamble Ernest Hochster took with a Western shirt in 1949 has paid off for the Hochster family and for customers of Western shirts.

For Collectors of Westmoor ★★★★★★★★★★★★★★★★★★

Panhandle Slim is one of the major Western shirt labels that developed independently of those based in Denver. Their 1950s special treatments are collectible, though there are not many on the market. Westmoor's design emphasis was on basic style, not on special features such as embroidery or appliqués.

Panhandle Slim Styling Guide:

—Late '40s to mid '50s: wool and rayon gabardines.

—Late '50s: 80/20 poly/cotton blend fabrics in solid colors. Super Ultra Vino; also 100 percent polyester Ultressa fabric.

—Early '60s: Fabric is sourced from Klopman, J. P. Stevens, and other non-Western fabric suppliers providing exclusive fabrics for Panhandle Slim.

—1974: A boom in button-shirt business shifts it from 60 percent snaps before 1974 to 75 percent buttons after.

—Mid '70s: Satins with fringe, two-tones, slash pockets; 65/35 poly/cotton blends; cotton chambray; wallpaper prints.

—Late '70s: early remakes Western shirts with fused collars.

—1990s and early '00s: Collections in the Panhandle Slim Western shirts group include the Brooks & Dunn Collection endorsed by Country music duo, Brooks & Dunn, and the Rough Stock Collection endorsed by rodeo star, Tuff Hedeman.

—2004: Vintage remakes with "Retro" designation in label and hangtags.

★★★★★★★★★★★★★★★★★★★★★★★★★★★★★★★★★★★★★

My sportsmen friends agree with me...There's no finer shirt than a Pendleton

● Sportsmen everywhere choose Pendleton shirts. Outdoor men prefer Pendleton Shirts because they give long, comfortable wear. The fabrics are virgin fleece wool, the highest quality obtainable. Exclusive patterns, styling, tailoring make a "Pendleton" a dress-up shirt as well as for rugged use outdoors. Insulate your body with a Pendleton virgin fleece wool shirt—then you'll always wear one for outdoors work and play. At the finer stores. $4.50 to $8.50. Pendleton Woolen Mills, Portland, Oregon.

No. 1290
Western Gambler
$8.50

Pendleton
America's finest 100% virgin fleece
WOOL SHIRTS

Reproduced on this page are eight
Sports Afield, New Yorker, Field & St
& Sportsman from June, 1936 to Fe
field of wool shirt prospects. Hur
customers, within a trading radius
for Pendleton Wool Shirts. . . B

ADVERTISE

Publication
Esquire
New Yorker
Field & Stream
Outdoor Life
Game Breeder & Sportsman
Sports Afield
Letters
TOTAL

OVER 3,750,0

CHAPTER 10

★ ★ ★ ★ ★ ★ ★ ★ ★ ★ ★

SIGNIFICANT OTHERS

Pendleton's "High-Grade Western Wear"

From its start as a manufacturer of wool blankets in 1909, Pendleton Woolen Mills has come to occupy a unique niche in the history of Western shirts. Pendleton, Oregon, was the wool-shipping center for the sheep-growing regions east of the Cascade Mountains at the end of the 1800s. In 1893, a scouring plant for wool being sent to markets in the eastern United States was built. When it went up for sale, Clarence and Roy Bishop, the sons of a retail merchant in Salem, Oregon, decided to buy it and build a modern woolen mill. The first Pendleton blankets were produced by the Bishops in 1909 for the nearby Nez Percé Indian reservation. Within a few years, they were expanding their market to include tribes in the Southwest. They were successful in these new markets because they incorporated colors and patterns preferred by the Native Americans. These so-called "Indian blankets" are still popular with consumers around the world and prized by collectors.

The family-owned company expanded production to additional mills and began making clothing in 1912 at a plant in Washougal, Washington. The Bishop's wool suitings and topcoats earned a reputation for quality in the men's market, and by the mid '20s, Pendleton Woolen Mills was manufacturing wool shirts. Their plain wool shirts were the garment of choice among loggers, farmers, and others who worked outside. Clarence Bishop, who had been running the Pendleton operations of the family's numerous mills, began weaving shirt fabric including the famous Pendleton virgin-wool plaid shirt, which got its start in the late 1920s.

While the Pendleton wool plaid shirt was a staple in the limited wardrobes of loggers, cowboys, and ranchers throughout the West, the company was beginning to experiment with different weaves and new patterns in the early '30s. Pendleton's first Western-style shirt, "The Western Gambler," appeared in 1937 as part of the company's gabardine/wool shirt line. Distinguishing

Left: Pendleton magazine ad run in black and white, 1936. Courtesy of Pendleton, Pendleton, Oregon.

design touches included four-button cuffs, pleated sleeves, diagonally cut pocket flaps, and six natural shell shank buttons on the front. The genuine shell buttons were said to be inspired by the shirts worn by cowboys in movies of the 1920s and '30s. By the early 1940s, Pendleton changed from natural shell to synthetic shank buttons. The Western Gambler is a full-cut shirt with a straight back yoke and center pleat and lined collar. It was Pendleton's only "Western" styled shirt for several decades and was frequently featured in advertisements for the company's entire shirt line in magazines throughout the country. Some of the ads featured the noted Western novelist Zane Grey.

It was 1951 before Pendleton ventured further into the Western apparel market with its "Pendleton Virgin Wool Sportswear and Westernwear" line. The group included Western-style pants but no shirts, not even the Western Gambler. It was not until fall 1976 that Western shirts were offered by Pendleton in its "Pendleton Westernwear" collection. Initially comprised of wool shirts, the line had expanded by 1979 to include numerous colors, styles, and fabrics. The Western shirts featured the longer shirttail characteristic of all Pendleton shirts. The longer tail prevented the shirt from creeping up to the waist of the wearer, a feature especially important to horseback riders.

The Pendleton Westernwear line was renamed "Pendleton High Grade Westernwear" in 1980. Two years earlier, Pendleton had introduced men's Western-style shirts in cotton and in polyester/cotton blends under the "PenWest" label. The group included long- and short-sleeve styles. The shank buttons used on the Western Gambler were replaced by synthetic pearl snaps. According to Pendleton designer Dave Bisset, these were the first "ombre" shaded plaids from the company. Bisset also designed the first Pendleton shirts with contrasting yokes in the late 1970s. The shirts featured snaps and pointed pocket flaps. Yoke treatments included conventional single-point front and back yokes as well as V-front yokes with angled flap pockets and double-pointed back yokes. Cottons and cotton/polyester blends were included in the fabric selection. In 1979, the PenWest label was replaced with the "PenWesterner" label, which continued to be produced into the 1980s.

Pendleton Woolen Mills is still owned and operated by descendents of the Bishop brothers. Pendleton Western-style shirts were produced at the Portland Garment Factory from 1936 until 1955. The shirt manufacturing operations were moved to the company's sewing plant in Milwaukie, Oregon, in 1956 and continued to be made there until 1997. Today the fabric continues to be woven in their Washougal, Washington, mill, but the shirts are produced in Mexico.

For Collectors of Pendleton ★★★★★★★★★★★★★★★★★★★★

Label Dating Guide

—The Western Gambler label in the late 1930s and 1940s was woven blue with gold lettering and sewn all around. The label reads, "Warranted to be a Pendleton" with "Pendleton" in large, fancy lettering. Other information on the label:

> TRADE MARK REG. U.S. PAT. OFF.
>
> PENDLETON WOOLEN MILLS
>
> PORTLAND, OREGON
>
> 100% VIRGIN WOOL

—Labels from 1979 are woven, stitched all around, with "Pendleton" in uppercase lettering across the top. Line two reads, "High grade Western wear." Lettering and art is black on a solid tan background. The "ball of yarn" registered wool logo also appears on the lower-lefthand corner of the label.

—Pendleton's 1981 PenWesterner label is woven and stitched all around with three lines of type separated by bars. Line one reads: "High grade Western wear." Line two: "PenWesterner." Line three: "Penwest, Portland, Oregon."

★★

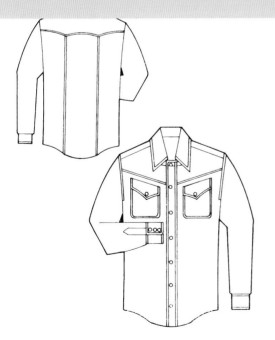

SPRING 1978

D070

MEN'S UMBRELLA BACK SHIRT

Placket front – shirt tail model
Snap front
Long sleeves – triple snap cuff
V-front yoke – bias cut
Two pockets – peaked flaps snap down and
   angled to yoke
Double peaked back yoke
Double track stitching detail
Self fabric yoke lined
Collar length – 3 3/4"
Packed – 2/12 per box

Sizing: Small (14–14½)   Medium (15–15½)
         Large (16–16½)   XLarge (17–17½)

Size Code: 9

Right: A Pendleton Western shirt line sheet, spring 1978. Courtesy of Pendleton, Pendleton, Oregon.

					UNIT COST	RETAIL PRICE
12	13	14	100% COTTON OXFORD			
–	–	–	D070-026	Blue	$12.50	$25.00
			D070-027	Tan		
			100% COTTON STRIPE			
			D070-028	Red/White	$12.50	$25.00

Above: A large, corrugated Wrangler/Blue Bell retail store mural, 1960–70s. Courtesy of Happy Days Vintage, Osaka, Japan.

Wrangler

Few Western apparel manufacturers have a more authentic claim to authentic American style than Wrangler. Even so, few companies in the business have more obscure beginnings, or a more uneven history as a collectible brand of Western shirt, despite a very distinguished pedigree.

Best known as a denim jeansmaker whose brand became synonymous with the American cowboy, Wrangler has also made shirts since the late 1940s. Most of the Western shirts from the '50s on were basic "work shirts for cowboys," as one Wrangler executive put it. With the possible exception of the company's signature denim snap shirt, the 27MW, Wrangler's shirt line is not considered particularly collectible. Indeed, Wrangler would not merit more than a brief note in the story of collectible Western shirts were it not for the role a famous custom designer had in its early history.

Wrangler got its start in 1905 when a work apparel manufacturer in Baltimore, Casey Jones, Inc., registered the name *Wrangler* as an apparel brand. Information about the company is sketchy, but it is known that the Wrangler brand was little used by the company.

Meanwhile, two brothers from Tennessee had acquired equipment from a Greensboro, North Carolina, manufacturer of work apparel where one of them worked until it closed in 1904. C. C. Hudson had sewn buttons on overalls at the factory since 1897. C. C. and his brother, Homer, bought some of the sewing machines and set up shop in Greensboro as the Hudson Overall Co. Indigo denim overalls were the staple in work apparel for the growing working class of Americans at the time. The Hudson brothers developed a thriving business catering to railroad workers.

In 1919, Hudson Overall was renamed Blue Bell Overall Co. According to legend, the name was in reference to a railroad bell given to the brothers by appreciative railroad customers. Over time, the bell was coated with fine blue dust from the indigo-colored denim being cut and sewn in the factory, hence the name Blue Bell and its well-known logo. In 1926, an ailing C. C. Hudson sold Blue Bell to a friendly rival, Big Ben Manufacturing, in Middlesboro, Kentucky. Big Ben headquarters moved to Greensboro and dropped the Big Ben name in favor of Blue Bell Overall Co. in 1930.

Through the early '30s as the Great Depression gripped America, Blue Bell Overall Co. became one of the biggest makers of work clothes. In 1936, it merged with rival Globe Superior Corporation of Abingdon, Illinois. Globe is credited with developing Sanforization, a manufacturing process that shrinks cloth before it is cut. The new company became Blue Bell-Globe Manufacturing Co. and remained headquartered in Greensboro. Blue Bell-Globe pioneered proportioned fit in the late '30s, a revolutionary concept that linked the rise in a pair of overalls to the length of its inseam. The innovation paved the way for further expansion. In 1943, Blue Bell-Globe acquired Casey Jones, Inc., along with its neglected brand name, Wrangler.

During World War II, Blue Bell-Globe was a major apparel contractor for the U.S. military. The company discovered that returning G.I.s had developed a liking for the khaki shirts and pants they had worn in the service, so the company added casual clothing to its line of work-related products. In 1947, the company purchased the Mid-South Garment Co., which had five shirt plants in

Mississippi. Blue Bell-Globe then adopted the slogan, "The World's Largest Producer of Work and Play Clothes." That year also marked the company's entrance into the Western apparel market. A year earlier, the company commissioned famed designer of custom costumes and clothes for cowboy movie stars and top rodeo hands, "Rodeo Ben," to design denim jeans for cowboys and ranchers.

Rodeo Ben's development of the famous Wrangler Cowboy Cut jean is well-documented and has been used heavily in Wrangler promotional materials since its introduction in 1947. Its unique place in the annals of Western apparel history—and in jeanswear in general—is built on style number 13MWZ, which is production shorthand for the thirteenth version of men's jeans with zipper. Rodeo Ben's contribution to Blue Bell's jeans business is interesting in light of the fact that he did not influence their shirt business, which was relegated to secondary importance for decades.

Blue Bell concentrated on basic Western shirts with yokes, flap pockets, and snaps. Perhaps the only collectible shirt from that era first appears in the 1947 Wrangler catalog—model number 27MW, the "Denim Plainsman Original Rodeo Cowboy Designed Shirt." The denim version of this shirt, which was also produced in chambray, became Wrangler's signature shirt from the 1950s to the '70s. According to former Wrangler president, Bill Hervey, "It had all the features a cowboy liked." He recalls, "It was form-fitting, it had extra-long tails that wouldn't come out of his jeans when he was on a horse, and it was durable—a great, all-around Western work shirt."

Legendary rodeo cowboy Jim Shoulders recalls that in 1947, Wrangler representatives showed up at a rodeo in Madison Square Garden in New York City with jeans and shirts for everybody involved with the rodeo. While he was impressed with the new jeans, Shoulders didn't much care for the shirt. "It was black with snaps on the pocket flaps and a Western-cut yoke," Shoulders recalls. "It also had 'Wrangler' stitched across the back yoke in two-inch yellow letters that made it look like a sign board. I told 'em I wouldn't wear a sign board."

Shoulders, who became a longtime Wrangler endorsee says that same shirt, without the objectionable name emblazoned across the back, came out in indigo denim a little later.

According to Hervey, who started with Blue Bell in 1957 as a sales representative for Wrangler, the shirts constituted "no more than 10 percent" of his sales to retailers. At the time,

Left: Wrangler cotton twill work shirt, 1970s. This basic work shirt is dated by its extremely long collar. Also features "W" pocket stitching and double needling. Courtesy of Brian Stratton, South Amboy, New Jersey.

the wholesale price of Wrangler shirts was about twenty-three dollars per dozen, which translated to about four dollars a shirt at retail. Today, the same kind of shirt wholesales for twenty-three dollars per shirt!

Wrangler shirts in the 1950s and '60s were plaids, prints, and plain styles, many of which were matching, so Mom, Dad, and the kids could all dress alike. For the most part, Wrangler Western shirts focused on the core, working cowboy and rodeo cowboy market with durable, basic, Western work shirts. "It wasn't a fashion item," explains Wrangler's unofficial archivist, Susan Downer. "We didn't do the different styles, it was a basic shirt."

By the '70s, Wrangler's shirt sales started to pick up. "When I was still on the road selling, we practically had to beg customers to buy them," Hervey says. "By then [in the '70s], I had gotten into management. I imagine that the sales of those shirts, particularly in the southwestern part of the country, and the far west, might have been 30 to 40 percent of the business." Buttons started appearing on Wrangler shirts in the '70s with the arrival of what Hervey terms, "fancy sports shirts" that were somewhat dressier.

A native Texan, Hervey traveled Texas and nearby states before being tapped for management. He served as president of Wrangler from 1981 until 1986, when Blue Bell, which became an employee-owned company in 1984 to avoid hostile takeovers, was acquired by VF Corporation. Hervey became Senior Vice President of Marketing, Wrangler Brand, for VF, a title he continues to hold.

Hervey recalls that the denim shirt was his best-selling shirt. "A lot of people called it the welder's shirt because people in the welding business bought that thing. Welders liked it because it didn't have any polyester in it, which would fry you if a spark hit it." He adds with a laugh that the designation was probably helped along because each pocket had yellow "W" stitching on each flap pocket, and people probably took that "W" to stand for welder, rather than Wrangler.

Joe Hertz, vice president and general manager for Wrangler shirts, says that the 27MW, and variations of it, is one of the most enduring shirt designs in the industry. "It's probably the biggest-selling shirt of any one shirt in the industry," he says.

He attributes part of its popularity to its starring status in movies and television programs over the years, and he believes *The Plainsman* was a significant inspiration for Ralph Lauren's repeated forays into Western design. "They may have laundered it or destroyed it, but the basic is that shirt," he says. "You go back to the *Six Million Dollar Man*, Lee Majors used to wear it all the time. Robert Redford wore it in *The Horse Whisperer*. He had that one and he also asked us to make him the green one that was really distressed. The celebrities really recognize it as a great shirt; it's Western, but it's also very contemporary."

Hertz, who joined Wrangler in 1979, says that the Urban Cowboy fad was a watershed event for the Western shirt industry and for Wrangler. "The biggest change really occurred in the late '70s, early '80s when Western shirts changed from being a uniform to an attitude," Hertz says.

BEAUTIFUL BODY,
NO UPKEEP,
ALL PARTS GUARANTEED.

This authentic Wrangler label is your guarantee of famous Wrangler Fashion.

Dacron˚ taffeta lining.

Permanent collar stays.

Single needle stitching.

Pencil slot.

Seven button (or snap) front.

Tailored sleeve placket

Proportioned, tapered waist.

All fabrics permanent press.

Tapered cuffs.

Fabrics pre-tested to insure strength, comfort, appearance and best fit.

Extra long tails.

Washing instructions and guarantee on permanent care label.

WRANGLER®
WESTERN WEAR
Wremember the "W" is Silent.

"Prior to the late '70s, probably 95 percent of all the Western shirts sold were snaps; 65 percent of that was stripes, plaids, and solids. They all had what we called the biased-Z formation where your yokes were angled one way, your [pocket] flaps were angled the other way, and the pockets the other way, and if you looked at it, it formed a 'Z'."

Classic Western styling like that gave way to more contemporary design and fabric choices as Wrangler discovered that young Western customers would buy their jeans, boots, and hats at the Western retail store, but go elsewhere to buy a shirt. "Kind of like their dads' Oldsmobile, they wanted something a little bit different," Hertz says. "At that time we started to pick up influences from the contemporary market in color, fabric, and silhouette, but we still kept touches of Western."

Those touches included pointed back yokes, extra-long tails, and Western-flavored packaging. But Wrangler revamped their shirt line significantly to court a new generation of consumers whose cultural and social influences differed dramatically from those of their parents. Shirt production also changed. The company began making shirts in Central America by the late '80s and have made shirts in Asia since the '90s.

For Collectors of Wrangler ★★★★★★★★★★★★★★★★★★

Label Dating Guide

—Wrangler shirts from the 1950s to the '70s feature the word *Wrangler* written in script on a plain white label, "Long Tails" in plain type and the words, "Made in U.S.A." at the bottom. Polyester and poly-blend shirts are designated with the words "PERMANENT PRESS" in capital letters on the label. Sizing tags are attached to the side of the label and indicate fabric content and neck and sleeve size.

—From about 1979 through the '80s, Wrangler labels include a galloping horse and "Wrangler" in block lettering on a colored background. Shirts in the Wrangler PRCA collection include the words "pro rodeo collection" on the label. Shirts made in the United States include a stitched star and the words, "Crafted with pride in USA," "Long tails," "Tapered fit," "Single needle tailoring." Neck and sleeve size or sports-shirt sizing also appear on labels. The fabric-content tag is sewn at the edge of the label.

★★★

Left: Wrangler ad, 1974. Features a Western shirt with buttons and a huge collar. Courtesy of Wrangler.

CHAPTER 11

★ ★ ★ ★ ★ ★ ★ ★ ★ ★ ★ ★ ★ ★

WESTERN SHIRT LABELS

If vintage shirts are art, labels are the signatures. A shirt without a label may be interesting but it is nameless, and like antique saddles, have less value without a maker's mark. The label says a lot about the brand.

When searching for vintage shirts, collector Katy K. of Ranch Dressing in Nashville says she always looks at the label first. She takes a fast glance at the overall garment, but her first in-depth look is at the label. The label is the point of reference, the hook on which every shirt is hung. A good label makes the shirt more interesting. Once she's registered the brand, she can go back and take in the finer details of the shirt.

The label tells the value the manufacturer put in its product. Good labels are woven and yarn-dyed. Better labels have thoughtfully designed graphics and colors. They look more expensive because they cost at least twice as much as cheaper printed labels. In today's figures, a good label costs almost a nickel and a cheap one costs a cent or less, depending on quantity. We are talking about pennies and fractions of a penny, but cheapness shows through and through.

A well-made product reflects pride even in its smallest details. How the label is attached also tells us about the garment and the brand. Better garments always have the labels sewn on all four edges. Stitching should not show on the back of the shirt. If stitching shows it means the label is an afterthought, added after manufacture. Such a shirt is not the manufacturer's primary brand; it is likely special-labeled for a chain store. A label sewn only on the ends is a cheaper operation that leaves the top and bottom loose. Still cheaper, labels can be set with glue or an iron. The label is the key to the brand, and the brand is as important as the design itself. Many collectors search for only certain brands. The label represents a commitment to quality and design.

Left: "Circle A WESTERN WEAR, tailored in California, Kohinoor Backbone Fabrics Vat Dyed Sanforized," 1940s. The neck and sleeve size tag are in the collar band. Courtesy of Kirsten Ehrig, California.

The label is a key clue to the age of the garment. Rockmount and H Bar C built long-term followings for certain designs that stayed in production for years, even decades. Designs that sold well went into production many times; some stayed in production indefinitely. Their labels, though, changed over the years as a way for brands to stay contemporary. Dating the label is critical to dating the designs that had long-term production runs.

The life cycle of a given style used to be longer. Today, styles tend to change every season. It has become unusual for a style to stay in production for an extended period. Even in the past, a style might go into production for one run, with a total of a few hundred pieces. The rarity of a style has to do with how long it remained in production. In terms of first-run commercially made shirts, the minimum most companies would produce is about 300 pieces, in up to three colorways of the same make. If this sold slowly, no more were made.

Labels give us a wide range of information, both stylistic and literal. Vintage labels often state selling points: "washable," "100 percent wool," "mercerized cotton," "made in U.S.A." Because styles, fonts, colors, and information changed over time, the label is a very good clue to the age of the shirt—like carbon-dating in archaeology.

However, the dating of the labels is an educated guess at best. And as the label helps date the garment, the garment helps date the label. Design elements of the shirt such as the style, fabric, collar, construction details, and special treatments help identify its date. Catalogs sometimes give us an exact year, but not the range of years a given label was in production.

Many brands produced goods with "special labels" (a different brand than the manufacturer's main label) for large-quantity customers. Often, special labels are deliberately unrelated to their main label to differentiate or hide the source. Sometimes the exact same garment was made under the main brand name but sold at higher prices to the independent stores. This was done especially for the chain stores that buy at discounted prices so that the independent stores were not selling the same exact thing at a higher price. It does not pertain to the highly collectible special designs because the discount chains did not carry stock in the higher-quality price range. These special label garments were usually produced in lower overall volume than their primary brands. They might have been used for a relatively short period of time, depending on the relationship between the supplier and the retailer.

Above: This printed label is from the 1940s–50s. The shirt features an enamel snap and contoured collar. Courtesy of Cookie Michael, Romancing the West, Houston, Texas.

Facing: "Fay Ward Co. Cowboy Tailors, NYC," 1940s. This custom-made wool gabardine shirt features a long fringe, chenille embroidery and rhinestones. Courtesy of Allan and Joyce Niederman, Chicago, Illinois.

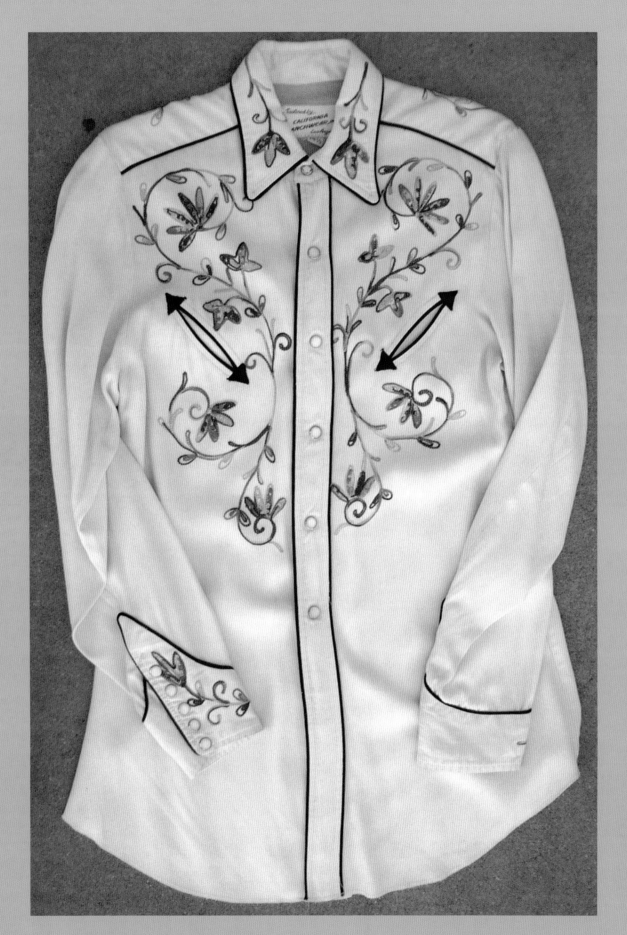

Left: H Bar C Ranchwear, men's gabardine with embroidery, 1950s. The high quality of this shirt is visible from the lined yoke to the woven label sewed on all four sides. The shirt also features smile pockets with sew on tabs, piping, and shot-gun cuffs. Courtesy of Candy's, Boulder, Colorado.

Another type of special label is when the manufacturer uses its recognizable brand name together with that of a good customer. This adds prestige for both the brand and the store. It is done for large orders prior to production so that the labels are sewn in during manufacture.

Finally, it has become common since the 1980s for retailers with multiple stores to produce their own special-label goods. These tend to be commodity-type styles, generally not collectible, highly stylized goods. It was fairly rare until the 1970s for stores to produce their own special-label shirts but has been more common since the 1980s. While there are special store labels from the early period, most of these retailers are long gone. It requires fairly large commitments, both financial and administrative, to produce your own merchandise. The minimums make it impractical except for staple goods.

Any quest for new labels will result in an appreciation for the diversity of brands made these last seventy years. Most people familiar with the Western shirt business might be able to come up with a dozen key brands. However, we unearthed about 250 different labels representing over 140 different brands. It is estimated that of those 140 brands, only twenty were in production long term. Of those twenty brands, just a few span fifty years or more. Just three brands have been in business the full seventy years that Western shirts have been in production.

It is one thing to have something made but an entirely different proposition to make it yourself. Some brands used contractors, others had their own factories. Those with factories tended to have, among other advantages, more flexibility in design. Most apparel companies today have closed their domestic factories and moved all their production to offshore contractors. This process has contributed to the homogenization of design and make, an intrinsic cultural loss. It is a sad irony to see the end of the domestic Western fashion industry, an American phenomenon.

Just as it took individualists like Henry Ford to create new automobile products and markets, it took individualists to create the diversity of brands that represent the history of Western shirts too. The domestic car business, which at one time numbered hundreds of different companies, is now consolidated to a relative few. Likewise, the Western shirt business is now consolidated so that the majority of shirts on the market come from only a few brands.

Something profound is lost as the market place goes from many to a few. The beauty of some of these labels is as significant as the shirts themselves. Some have history we know; others just leave us a name by which to remember their contribution to classic American fashion.

If vintage shirts are art, labels are the signatures.

The following pages list, in alphabetical order, all the Western shirt labels we could find in the United States, Europe, and Japan, from early to contemporary, tailor-made to commercial. Beneath each label is an upper and lowercase-sensitive description, and estimated date of production.

Levi, Pendleton, and Miller were the earliest makers of transitional style Western shirts, beginning in the 1930s. Levi and Pendleton dropped Western shirts for decades, although they later returned to the market. Miller made Western shirts the longest, but dropped the Miller label in favor of other brands in the 1980s. H Bar C was the second-oldest company in the Western business, but did not make Western shirts until the 1940s. At that point they used the brand continuously until the company's demise in 1999. The Rockmount brand was introduced in 1946 and is the longest continuously used Western label. The Wrangler shirt brand and Westmoor's Panhandle Slim brand date from the late 1940s and continue still. Karman, in business since 1947, produced various labels, dropping the Karman label in favor of others in the 1990s.

"101, one-o-one," 1930s. Brand belonging to the world-famous Oklahoma ranch, possibly licensed to Miller & Co. Courtesy of Traditions West, Cody, Wyoming.

"AMERICAN HERO AUTHENTIC SHIRTS," 1980s. Courtesy of Candy's Vintage, Boulder, Colorado.

"ANNA ZAPP DESIGNS," 1970–80s. Standardized "L" sizing. Anna Zapp is most famous for designing stage clothing for the likes of John Denver and was based out of Boulder, Colorado.

"Arizona Original, TUCSON ARIZONA," custom-made for Jack Navin, 1950s. Courtesy of The Collection of Thomas Oatman Labels.

"ARIZONA Wilson Brothers," 1950s.

"Authentic WESTERN RANCHWEAR," 1960s. Made by H Bar C. Courtesy of Dan Shapiro, Southwest, Ltd., Costa Mesa, California.

"Authentic WESTERN RANCHWEAR," 1960s. Made by H Bar C. Courtesy of La Rosa Vintage Boutique, San Francisco, California.

"AUTHENTIC WESTERN WEAR," 1970s. H Bar C import line. Courtesy of Dan Shapiro, Southwest, Ltd., Costa Mesa, California.

"Avante West," 1970–80s. Courtesy of Used Clothing Daikanyama, Tokyo, Japan.

"BEN THE RODEO TAILOR, 5209 W. COLUMBIA AVE., PHILADELPHIA, PA," 1940s. Courtesy of Cowboy Story Land & Cattle Co, Cody, Wyoming. See also "Rodeo Ben" label, page 157.

"Bert Pulitzer, Tom Bass," 1970–80s. Courtesy of Nelda's Vintage, San Antonio, Texas.

"BIG MAC," 1980s. Courtesy of Aaardvark's Odd Ark, San Francisco, California.

"BJ-R Authentic Western Shirt, LONG TAIL FORM-FIT," 1970–80s. Tape label includes The "L" size sewn into collar band, saves two operations. Courtesy of Voice Vintage, Daikanyama,Tokyo, Japan.

"Border Town AUTHENTIC WESTERN SHIRT, LONG TAIL FORM-FIT, PERMANENT PRESS," 1970s. "Authentic" but made in Korea! Size tag includes neck and sleeve sizing. Courtesy of Nelda's Vintage, San Antonio, Texas.

"'Botany' Natural Wool Loomed in America, certified by Chatham," 1970s. Courtesy of La Rosa Vintage Boutiqe, San Francisco, California.

"BRONCO AUTHENTIC WESTERN, FORM FIT, LONG TAIL, DURABLE PRESS," 1970s. Keeping the washing instructions and size on the label saves two operations, and side stitching the tag saves money.

"Styled by BUCK SKEIN JOE, TRADE MARK," 1940–50s. Courtesy of The Collection of Thomas Oatman Labels.

"Bud Bermu Westerner," 1970–80s. Courtesy Nelda's Vintage, San Antonio, Texas.

"Tailored by CALIFORNIA RANCH-WEAR, Los Angeles," 1940–50s. Later this brand became H Bar C. Courtesy of La Rosa Vintage Boutique, San Francisco, California.

"Tailored by CALIFORNIA RANCH-WEAR, Los Angeles," 1940–50s. The neck and sleeve size tag hangs below. Being washable was a big selling point.

"Tailored by CALIFORNIA RANCH-WEAR, Los Angeles, WASH IN LUKE WARM SOAP SUDS, PRESS WITH COOL IRON," 1940s–50s. Bust size tag says "34."

"Tailored by CALIFORNIA RANCH-WEAR, Inc., Los Angeles, MADE IN U.S.A.," 1970s or later. Courtesy of Dan Shapiro, Southwest, Ltd., Costa Mesa, California.

"Champion Westerns Permanent Press," 1970–80s. This import line based in Denver was owned by Don Handler, who had worked previously for Karman.

"rugged outdoor wear, carhartt," 1980s. Tape label. Courtesy of Fine Clothing Daddy, Osaka, Japan.

"Char designs, SANTA FE," 1980s.
Bust size "38" is sewn in on the side.

"CHUTE #1."

"Circle A WESTERN WEAR, tailored in
California. Kohinoor Backbone
Fabrics Vat Dyed Sanforized," 1940s.
Neck and sleeve size tag in collar
band. Courtesy of Kirsten Ehrig,
California.

"RODEO SHIRT by Conqueror," 1950s.
Courtesy of The Collection of Thomas
Oatman Labels.

"LAS VEGAS by Cowboy Joe, FORM-
FIT HAND WASHABLE," 1950–60s.
Washability and fit were selling
points. Courtesy of The Collection
of Thomas Oatman Labels.

"Cowboy Joe, GUARANTEED WASH-
ABLE, WESTERN STYLE," 1940–50s.

"Cowboy Joe USE MILD SOAP—COOL
IRON," 1940–50s. Courtesy of The
Collection of Thomas Oatman Labels.

"LAS VEGAS AUTHENTIC WESTERN
SHIRT by Cowboy Joe, FORM FIT,"
1950–60s.

"DC, DEE CEE BRAND PERMANENT
PRESS AUTHENTIC WESTERN WEAR
BY WASHINGTON MFG. CO., MADE IN
USA," 1970s.

"WASHINGTON 'DEE-CEE' WESTERN
WEAR," 1960s. Made by Washington
Mfg. Co.

"DeeCee Rangers, PERMANENT PRESS,
WASHINGTON MFG. CO., MADE IN U.S.A.,
Mr. Tall," 1980s. This shirt's selling
points were its tall fit and permanent
press. Courtesy of Aaardvark's Odd
Ark, San Francisco, California.

"THE DENVER SHIRT, DENVER,
COLORADO USA," 1970s.

"CUSTOM MADE DIAMOND SHIRT 105 E. SUNSET BLVD, LOS ANGELES, CALIF.," 1940s. Courtesy of Willow Springs Antique Mall, Cody, Wyoming.

"FRONT UNION DEPOT CUSTOM MADE DIAMOND SHIRT 105 E. SUNSET BLVD, LOS ANGELES, CALIF.," 1940s.

"Lady DJ by Dickson-Jenkins," 1980s. Courtesy of Junk Vintage, Osaka, Japan.

"QUALITY SUPREME, D-J, ALL COTTON, DICKSON-JENKINS MFG. CO.," 1950–60s.

"STYLED BY Don Juan MADE IN CALIFORNIA," 1950s. The early "S" sizing in label saves one operation. Courtesy of Aaardvark's Odd Ark, San Francisco, California.

"Double S WESTERNS, PERMANENT PRESS, EXTRA LONG TAIL," 1970–80s. An inexpensive make with tape label, including standard sizing tag sewn into collar band. Courtesy of Nelda's Vintage, San Antonio, Texas.

"DR WESTERNS, FABRICS BY DAN RIVER," 1970–80s. Dan River is a textile manufacturer that appears in many labels.

"Dunfield Western Wear, J.M. McDonald CO.," 1957. From the Miller & Co. Catalog. Courtesy of Miller International, Denver, Colorado.

"The Plains by E&W, FORM-FIT," 1950–60s. Made by Ely Walker.

"FIBER/CARE OTHER SIDE ELY PLAINS MADE IN USA SINCE 1878," 1970–80s. The neck and sleeve size appear on the same label, saving two operations.

"ELY PLAINS RIDER," 1970s. Courtesy of Funky Monkey Vintage, New Orleans, Louisiana.

"FAY WARD CO. COWBOY TAILORS 306 WEST 48th St., N.Y.C.," 1940s. Custom-made shirt, courtesy of Allan and Joyce Niederman, Chicago, Illinois.

"FENTON PERMANENT PRESS, EXTRA LONG TAIL," 1970s. Sewing the tape label in collar band seam saves an operation. Import line owned by Sonny Handler, who worked previously for Tem-Tex. Courtesy of Cody Antique Mall, Cody, Wyoming.

"LONG TAIL WESTERNER by Fleetline FORM-FIT," 1950–60s. Early "L" sizing in label saves an operation. Courtesy of Fine Clothing Daddy Vintage, Osaka, Japan.

"Frontier SHIRT MADE IN CALIFORNIA," 1940s. Neck size tag hangs below label. Courtesy of Ronny Weiser, Las Vegas, Nevada.

"GAME AND LAKE Sportswear EXPERTLY TAILORED," 1930–40s. A transitional Western, whose label was later bought by Westmoor. Courtesy of Rockmount, Denver, Colorado.

"GURANTEED Glover QUALITY," 1920–30s. An early wool pullover. Courtesy of David Little, Cody Antique Mall, Cody, Wyoming.

"Goatroper by PMC MADE IN U.S.A.," 1970s. Courtesy of Hex Hiue Vintage, Nara, Japan.

"GRAND CANYON," 1970s.

"GREAT WESTERN, A PRODUCT OF THE REAL NORTH WEST, DRY CLEAN ONLY DO NOT WASH," 1940s.

"Another Original Westerner tailored by Harris Tailoring Co., FORT WORTH, TEXAS," 1940–50s. Courtesy of the National Cowboy & Western Heritage Museum, Oklahoma City, Oklahoma.

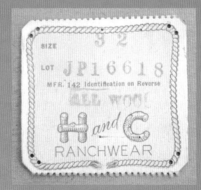

"H and C RANCHWEAR" paper pant tag, 1930s. This is an early logo, prior to H BAR C. Courtesy of Dan Shapiro, Southwest, Ltd., Costa Mesa, California.

"H BAR C RANCH WEAR CA," 1940s. A very early tag in lariat. Note that Ranch Wear is two words. Courtesy of the National Cowboy & Western Heritage Museum, Oklahoma City, Oklahoma.

"H BAR C RANCHWEAR," 1950s. This is a rare, variegated, early small label. Courtesy of Brian Stratton, South Amboy, New Jersey.

"Tailored Originals, the Frontex Co., DALLAS," 1940–50s. Courtesy of Aaardvark's Odd Ark, San Francisco, California.

"H BAR C RANCHWEAR, ALL WOOL," 1950s. Used in shirts and suitings. Courtesy of Dan Shapiro, Southwest, Ltd., Costa Mesa, California.

"H BAR C, CAL-RANCH," 1950s. A large label—2.5 x 2 inches— for suitings and shirts. Courtesy of Dan Shapiro, Southwest, Ltd., Costa Mesa, California.

"H BAR C, CALIFORNIA RANCHWEAR," 1950s. A large label for suiting and shirts. Courtesy of Dan Shapiro, Southwest, Ltd., Costa Mesa, California.

"H BAR C RANCHWEAR in Celanese 'Lustrocel,'" 1950s. Courtesy of Brian Stratton, South Amboy, New Jersey.

"H BAR C RANCHWEAR, WASHABLE, Exclusive Design," 1950s. Women's bust size "40" stamped in collar band predates size tags. Courtesy of Dan Shapiro, Southwest, Ltd., Costa Mesa, California.

H Bar C Ranchwear, 1950–80s. Four women's and children's tape labels. Courtesy of Dan Shapiro, Southwest, Ltd., Costa Mesa, California.

H Bar C Ranchwear hang tags: tan with hole for snap, 1960s; Wrink-l-less, 1970–80s; blue ribbon, 1970–80s; gold, 1980s; pen slot, 1960–70s; hanger decal, 1960s. Courtesy of Dan Shapiro, Southwest, Ltd., Costa Mesa, California.

"H BAR C RANCHWEAR, CALIFORNIA RANCHWEAR, EL DORADO COLLECTION, 1970s. Label is 2 x 2 inches. Courtesy of Dan Shapiro, Southwest, Ltd., Costa Mesa, California.

"H BAR C RANCHWEAR, CALIFORNIA RANCHWEAR," 1970s. Label is 2 x 1.75 inches. Courtesy of Dan Shapiro, Southwest, Ltd., Costa Mesa, California.

"Hi-Sierra H BAR C CAL RANCHWEAR MADE IN USA," 1970s. Courtesy of Dan Shapiro, Southwest, Ltd., Costa Mesa, California.

"H BAR C RANCHWEAR, TAILORED EXPRESSLY FOR Jeferman's," 1970–80s. Courtesy of Dan Shapiro, Southwest, Ltd., Costa Mesa, California.

"H BAR C RANCHWEAR Long Tail, MADE IN U.S.A.," 1980s. Courtesy of Dan Shapiro, Southwest, Ltd., Costa Mesa, California.

"H BAR C RANCHWEAR, MADE IN U.S.A.," 1980s. Courtesy of Dan Shapiro, Southwest, Ltd., Costa Mesa, California.

"H BAR C RANCHWEAR MADE EXPRESSLY FOR WESTERN WORLD, THE WORLD'S LARGEST CHAIN OF WESTERN STORES," 1970–80s. Courtesy of Dan Shapiro, Southwest Ltd., Costa Mesa, California.

"H BAR C RANCHWEAR CAL RANCH-WEAR Hi-Sierra," 1970–80s. This was a large jacket label, 2.5 x 2 inches. Courtesy of Dan Shapiro, Southwest, Ltd., Costa Mesa, California.

"H BAR C CALIFORNIA RANCHWEAR MADE IN U.S.A.," 1970–90s. This is their most common later label. Courtesy of Dan Shapiro, Southwest, Ltd., Costa Mesa, California.

"H bar C DESIGNER COLLECTION, MADE IN U.S.A.," 1990s. Courtesy of Dan Shapiro, Southwest, Ltd., Costa Mesa, California.

"H BAR C, CALIFORNIA RANCHWEAR, MADE IN U.S.A.," 1990s. Courtesy of Dan Shapiro, Southwest, Ltd., Costa Mesa, California.

"H BAR C, CALIFORNIA RANCHWEAR, MADE IN USA," 1980–90s. Courtesy of Dan Shapiro, Southwest, Ltd., Costa Mesa, California.

"CUSTOM TAILORED TO MEASURE, Herbert, Cincinnati, DRY CLEAN ONLY DO NOT WASH," 1940–50s. Courtesy of La Rosa Vintage Boutique, San Francisco, California.

"HIDACO, WASHABLE, MADE IN JAPAN," 1950s. Courtesy of Dan Shapiro, Southwest Ltd., Costa Mesa, California.

"Hilbilly Westerns, Denver," 1940–50s. Courtesy of Cowgirls of the West Museum, Cheyenne, Wyoming.

"Holt, Quality Western Wear," 1970–80s. Label sewn into collar-band seam.

"HOMBRE CALIFORNIA AUTHENTIC WESTERN SHIRT," 1970–80s. Tape label includes "M" sizing sewn into collar seam, saving two operations.

"HORIZON, FULLY WASHABLE," 1950s. Being washable was a big selling point. Neck and sleeve sizing are part of the label. Courtesy of **The Collection of Thomas Oatman Labels.**

"HOOFS," 1970–80s. Courtesy of Full Up Vintage, Daikanyama, Tokyo, Japan.

"HOOT-SPAH WESTERNS," 1970–80s. A clever play on words. The tape label is sewn into the collar band saving a separate operation. Courtesy of Full Up Vintage, Daikanyama, Tokyo, Japan.

"THE HUSTLER COLLECTION," 1970s. Courtesy of Full Up Vintage, Daikanyama, Tokyo, Japan.

"J Bar J REG. WESTERN WEAR, California Made," 1940–50s. This is a printed label. Courtesy of Cookie Michael, Romancing the West, Houston, Texas.

"Jason, MADE IN USA by Fantasia," 1970–80s. A brand that catered to square dancers.

"JACK FROST WOOLEN WEAR, The Original UTAH WOOLEN MILL, SALT LAKE CITY," 1930–50s. Side tag reads: DO NOT WASH DRY CLEAN ONLY. Courtesy of Jacqueline Strong, Gordon, Nebraska.

"JOHN'S CUSTOM SHIRTS, PHOENIX, ARIZONA," June, 1961. Custom-made for Glenn Randall, the Hollywood horse trainer who trained Trigger. Courtesy of the National Cowboy & Western Heritage Museum, Oklahoma City, Oklahoma.

"FORM FITTED KARMAN, DENVER, COL-ORADO, Western Shirts," 1950–60s. Neck and sleeve size tag is sewn in the collar band. Courtesy of Traditions West Antiques, Cody, Wyoming.

"KARMAN," 1980s. Features stitched sides only and size tag in the collar-band seam.

"Silver Collection by KARMAN," 1970–80s. Features stitched sides only.

"Kenny Rogers WESTERN COLLEC-TION by Karman," 1980s. Features stitched sides only.

"Kenny Rogers WESTERN COLLECTION BY KARMAN," 1980s. Features stitched sides only. Courtesy of Ronny Weiser, Las Vegas, Nevada.

"LOONEY TUNES WESTERN COLLECTION BY KARMAN," 1990s. This is a printed label with stitched sides only.

"Katy K DESIGNS, NEW YORK," 1980–1995. Courtesy of Ranch Dressing, Nashville, Tennessee.

"Katy K Designs," 1995–present. Courtesy of Ranch Dressing, Nashville, Tennessee.

"KAUFFMAN RIDING GOODS STORE, 141 EAST 24th ST. N.Y.," 1940s. In business from 1875–1996, now Kauffman.com. Courtesy of Santa Monica Vintage, Tokyo, Japan.

"Koman, MADE IN KOREA," 1970–80s. An inexpensive cotton/poly blend with a tape label including standard sizing, sewn into collar band. Courtesy of Nelda's Vintage, San Antonio, Texas.

"Larry Mahan's Wild WEST," 1970s. Made in Mexico, this label is sewn into the collar band with the size tag under it. Courtesy of Osaka Vintage, Osaka, Japan.

"Larry Mahan, MACHINE WASH WARM," 1980s. This tape label includes the care instructions and is sewn into the collar band.

"LEVI STRAUSS Rodeo Shirt," 1930–40s. Courtesy of Ronny Weiser, Las Vegas, Nevada.

"LEVI STRAUSS, MAKERS OF LEVI'S OVERALLS AUTHENTIC WESTERN WEAR, DRY CLEAN ONLY," 1930–40s. Courtesy of Scott Corey, Santa Fe, New Mexico.

"LEVI'S AUTHENTIC WESTERN WEAR, LEVI STRAUSS of CALIFORNIA," 1950–60s.

"LEVI'S AUTHENTIC WESTERN WEAR, LEVI STRAUSS & CO., SAN FRANCISCO," 1960s. Side stitched only. Courtesy of Nobu Hirota, Johnny Angel/Cactus Blues, Osaka, Japan.

"LI'L HOMBRE Nattyboy," 1950s. Courtesy of Steve Weil, Denver, Colorado, and David Little, Traditions West, Cody, Wyoming.

"THE Little Champ OF HOLLYWOOD, MADE IN CALIFORNIA," 1950s. A child's sport collar. Courtesy of Nobu Hirota, Johnny Angel/Cactus Blues, Osaka, Japan.

"DESIGNED & TAILORED by Maude McMorries, DOOLE, TEXAS," 1960s. Courtesy of the National Cowboy & Western Heritage Museum, Oklahoma City, Oklahoma.

"MARGUCCI," 1970–80s. Courtesy of Nelda's, San Antonio, Texas.

"Country & Outdoors from Marlboro Classics, QUALITY LABEL," 1980–90s. A woven "Large" size tag hangs below. Courtesy of VMC Jeans Store, Zurich, Switzerland.

"Matchless, SUPERFINE GABARDINE," 1940–50s. Courtesy of Santa Monica Vintage, Tokyo, Japan.

"MAYFAIR, LOS ANGELES, BEVERLY HILLS, HOLLYWOOD," 1940s. Courtesy of David Little, Cody Antique Mall, Cody, Wyoming.

"MILLER Western Wear DENVER COLORDO, 100% ALL WOOL," 1930–40s. Shirt predates size tags. Courtesy of Jack A. Weil, Denver, Colorado.

"MILLER, DENVER COLO, FINE SHIRTS, MADE IN U.S.A.," 1930s. This was early on when being made in the U.S.A. was a selling point, and before size tags. Courtesy of Susan Adams.

"MILLER Western Wear, DENVER COLORADO," 1940s. Features a "Second" stamp.

"MILLER Western Wear, DENVER COLORADO," 1950s.

"MILLER, Western Wear, DENVER COLORADO," 1960s. This shirt was styled in the West for a true Western cut and fit, but made in Japan. Courtesy of Ronny Weiser, Las Vegas, Nevada.

"MILLER, Western Wear, DENVER COLORADO," 1960s.

"MILLER Ride Em Cowboy, DENVER COLORADO," "WASH AND WEAR, LITTLE IRONING NEEDED," 1960s. Courtesy of Candy's Vintage, Boulder, Colorado.

"Miller Sportswear, MACHINE WASH-ABLE," and hangtag, 1960–70s. This is a boy's shirt. Courtesy of Broadway Review, Denver, Colorado.

"miller miller miller, western wear, denver colorado," 1970s. Courtesy of Junk Vintage, Osaka, Japan.

"millie," 1970s. A Miller women's label. Courtesy of Happy Days Vintage, Osaka, Japan.

"miller westernwear, Denver, Colo, USA," 1970–80s. The neck and sleeve size tag is in collar band.

"Murdock's WESTERN STYLES, RENO, NEVADA." The shirt size and "WASH-FAST," the selling point, are stamped on collar band, predating size tags. Courtesy of Aardvark's Odd Ark, San Francisco, California.

"MUSTANG," 1970s.

"MUSTANG, LONG TAIL FORM FIT, WASHABLE, MADE IN U.S.A.," 1970s. Also has a long collar! Courtesy of Hex Hiue Vintage, Nara, Japan.

"MWG, johnny west, CANADA," 1970–80s. A tape label sewn into the collar band. Courtesy of Cowboy Story Land & Cattle Co., Cody, Wyoming.

"N. Turk, 13175 VENTURA BLVD, VAN NUYS, CALIF., Individually Styled," 1940s. Courtesy of La Rosa Vintage Boutique, San Francisco, California.

"New Era OUT O' DOORS WITH LINE-FOLD COLLAR," 1940–50s. Courtesy of The Collection of Thomas Oatman Labels.

"NORTHERN PLAINS SHIRT COMPANY,"
1970–80s. Made in Korea.

"Old Kentucky, WELL MADE, WEST-
ERN WEAR, MADE IN U.S.A. PERMA-
NENT PRESS," 1960s. The neck and
sleeve size tag is woven and sewed
in the collar band.

"OPEN TRAILS," 1970–80s. Courtesy
of Funky Monkey Vintage, New
Orleans, Louisiana.

"The Painted Desert Brand OF
ARIZONA—PRESCOTT," 1950–60s.
From the women's line. Courtesy of
Willow Springs Antique Mall, Cody,
Wyoming.

"Panhandle Slim SUPER FORM-FIT, A
Westmoor PRODUCT," 1950–60s.
Printed label. Courtesy of Nobu
Hirota, Johnny Angel/Cactus Blues,
Osaka, Japan.

"Panhandle Slim SUPER FORM-FIT, A
Westmoor PRODUCt," 1960s. Label is
identical to previous label, but is
woven, not printed.

"Panhandle Slim, A Westmoor PROD-
UCT, SUPER FORM-FIT, TAILORED for
LOU TAUBERT RANCH OUTFITTERS
Corral O Famous Brands, CASPER,
WYO.," 1950s. Private label on a lined,
reinforced collar band. Courtesy of
Cody Antique Mall, Cody, Wyoming.

"WESTERN TRENDS by Panhandle
Slim, PROUD TO BE AMERICAN,"
1970s. Has a neck and sleeve sizing
label. Courtesy of Junk Vintage,
Osaka, Japan.

"Ranch and Town by Panhandle
Slim," 1970–80s. This is a printed
label, sewn on the side seams only,
with a neck and sleeve size tab.

"THE PANHANDLER, LONG TAIL, FORM
FIT, Washable, MADE IN U.S.A.,"
1959–60s. Courtesy of The Collection
of Thomas Oatman Labels.

"PARDNERS," 1980s. Made in China,
and has standardized "M" sizing.

"Pendleton, HIGH GRADE WESTERN
WEAR, PENDLETON WOOLEN MILLS,
PORTLAND, OREGON, 100% VIRGIN
WOOL," 1979. Courtesy of Pendleton,
Pendleton, Oregon.

"HIGH GRADE WESTERN WEAR, PenWesterner, PENWEST, PORT-LAND, OREGON," 1981. Courtesy of Pendleton, Pendleton, Oregon.

"WARRNTED TO BE A 'PENDLETON,' PENDLETON WOOLEN MILLS, PENDLE-TON OREGON, 100% VIRGIN WOOL," 1930–40s. This shirt is an example of the transitional Western style. Courtesy of Steve Weil, Denver, Colorado.

"PENNEY'S FOREMOST SANFORIZED," 1950s. Printed, glued label. Courtesy of Pigsty Vintage, Osaka, Japan.

"Peter's SPORT CENTER, DETROIT," 1940s. Courtesy of Cowboy Story Land & Cattle Co., Cody, Wyoming.

"Pilgrim Westerner," 1950–60s. Size and "washfast" washability stamped on collar band. This is possibly a Miller & Co. special label. It was featured in Miller catalogs between 1961 and '62.

"EST 1993, RR RALPH LAUREN," 1990s. Shirt was made in Singapore and has standardized "M" sizing.

"FRONTIER FASHIONS, PORTER'S, PHOENIX TUCSON," 1940–50s. An early label on a transitional/Western style shirt. Courtesy of Santa Monica Vintage, Tokyo, Japan.

"Frontier Fashions PORTERS Phoenix, Tucson," 1950s.

"A GREAT FIT . . . A GREAT SHIRT, The PORTER SHIRT, STYLED BY PORTERS OF ARIZONA," 1960s. The neck and sleeve sizing is stitched in the label.

"Frontier Fashions, PORTER'S, PHOENIX, TUCSON," 1940s. Courtesy of The Collection of Thomas Oatman Labels.

"PRIOR, DENVER," 1940s. An early label; size stamp is in collar band. Courtesy of the National Cowboy & Western Heritage Museum, Oklahoma City, Oklahoma.

"Prior, Denver," 1940–50s.

"RRW Distinctive Rockmount Ranch Wear Mfg. Co., DENVER COLO., CUSTOM FITTED," 1950s. Features an early size tag. Courtesy of Rockmount, Denver, Colorado.

This Prior model and size stamp on the shirttail predates size tags; 1940s. Note the inexpensive surged tail; given the expensive embroidered make, one would expect a hemmed tail. Courtesy of La Rosa Vintage Boutique, San Francisco, California.

"PRIOR, Spun Rayon, GABARDINE," 1940s.

"PRIOR, DENVER, DRY CLEAN ONLY," 1940–50s. Courtesy of the National Cowboy & Western Heritage Museum, Oklahoma City, Oklahoma.

"BIGHORN, 100% VIRGIN WOOL, PRIOR, DENVER," 1940–50s. Features a transitional Western style. Courtesy of La Rosa Vintage Boutique, San Francisco, California.

"PRIOR Westerns, DENVER," 1970s. A tape label sewn in the collar-band seam. Courtesy of Junk Vintage, Osaka, Japan.

"PRIOR, DENVER, HAND WASHABLE," 1940s–50s. Courtesy of The Collection of Thomas Oatman Labels.

"PRYDE," 1970–80s. This is an ironic brand name given its glued, least-expensive label. Courtesy of Nelda's Vintage, San Antonio, Texas.

"Psycho Cowboy Brand, Scandinavian System, Active Sport and Streetwear," 2002. A recent label from Denmark. Courtesy of Scream, Daikanyama, Tokyo, Japan.

"R -BAR- S Authentic Western," 1970s. Includes a neck and sleeve sizing tab.

"RANCH-MAID WESTERN WEAR, DEN-VER," 1950s. A women's line made by Hilb Co. Ruddock bought the label in the 1960s. Courtesy of David Little, Cody Antique Mall, Cody, Wyoming.

"RANCH-MAN WESTERNWEAR, DEN-VER, 1950–60s. Part of a men's line made by Hilb Co. Ruddock bought the label in the 1960s.

"RANCHO by Bluestone, FULLY WASHABLE," 1950s. The shirt's selling point, its washability, is on the label, as are the sleeve and neck sizing.

"RANGELAND, TAILORED BY WILSON BROTHERS, DRY CLEAN ONLY," 1940s. A transitional style shirt.

"Rock Creek Ranch," 1970–80s. An imported brand. Courtesy of Funky Monkey Vintage, New Orleans, Louisiana.

"ROCKING K RANCHWEAR, BY KEN-NINGTON," 1970s. This printed label was sewn into the collar band, saving an operation.

"RRW Rockmount Ranch Wear, DEN-VER COLO., WASHABLE," mid-1940s. This rare label includes its selling point on the label. This shirt is part of the Rockmount collection courtesy of the Governor Sweet family, Colorado.

"RRW Rockmount Ranch Wear, DENVER COLO., ORIGINAL MODEL," mid 1940s. The men's neck and sleeve size collar stamp predates size tags, which were introduced in 1954. Courtesy of Rockmount, Denver, Colorado.

"RRW Rockmount Ranch Wear, DENVER COLO., ORIGINAL MODEL," mid–1940s. Features a women's bust size "34" collar stamp. The star-shaped ink stamp on the label signifies a factory second. Courtesy of Rockmount, Denver, Colorado.

"Celanese* Flannese*, A RAYON FABRIC, LAUNDER BY WOOL METHOD," mid-1940s. A special Rockmount label with additional information.

"RRW Rockmount Ranch Wear, DENVER COLO., WASHABLE," 1940s. Women's shirt, bust size "34," and form-fit collar stamp. Courtesy of Rockmount, Denver, Colorado.

"RRW Rockmount Ranch Wear, DEN-VER COLO., WASHABLE," mid-1950s. Early offset-printed size tag, bell-shaped hang tag, and collar sticker.

"RRW Wrinkl–SHED, Rockmount Ranch Wear, DENVER, COLO., IT'S A DAN RIVER FABRIC," 1950s. The size tag includes the model name and number and neck and sleeve sizes.

Rockmount Ranch Wear Mfg. Co. bell-shaped hang tag, a "Dan River Wrinkle–SHED with Dri–Don" hang tag, and a retail sales receipt for $6.95 from the 1950s. Dan River fabrics and fabrics with fewer wrinkles were big selling points.

"RRW TRU–WEST Rockmount Ranch Wear Mfg. Co., DENVER, COLO., CUS-TOM FITTED" with premium interlining ("There's PELLON Inside"), mid 1970s–1989. The label intentionally raveled when washed so it could not be sold again as new.

"RRW TRU—WEST Rockmount Ranch Wear Mfg. Co., DENVER, COLO., MADE IN U.S.A.," 1989–present.

The "RRW" navy cuff tab is on every Rockmount shirt created since 1975. Rockmount was granted a special U.S. trademark for the positioning and brand.

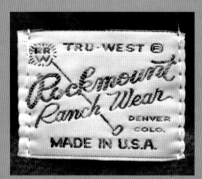

The classic variegated label was re-introduced for premium fabrics and the vintage collection in the 1990s and continues to the present. The remake version can be distinguished from original by the new "Made in U.S.A."

"Rodeo Ben, PHILADELPHIA, PA," 1940s. Courtesy of The Collection of Thomas Oatman Labels. See also "Ben the Rodeo Tailor," page 140.

"GENUINE ROEBUCKS, MACHINE WASH WARM, LINE OR TUMBLE DRY . . .," 1970–80s. Including the care instructions and standard "S" sizing on the label, saves an operation.

"Roper," 1940–50s. Made by Karman. Courtesy of Karman, Denver, Colorado.

"Round-up, LONG TAIL, FORM FIT, Washable, MADE IN U.S.A.," 1960s. Courtesy of Karman, Denver, Colorado.

Round—up cuff tag, 1960s. Made by Karman.

"Roy Rogers, 'Trigger,' 'King of the Cowboys,'" 1950s. Courtesy of The Collection of Thomas Oatman Labels.

"RUDDOCK Shirts" and U.S. flag side tab, 1968–present. Courtesy of Nelda's Vintage, San Antonio, Texas.

"FLYING R RANCHWEAR BY RUDDOCK MFG. CO., EL PASO, TEXAS," 1980s. A neck and sleeve sizing tag hangs beneath. Courtesy of Nelda's Vintage, San Antonio, Texas.

"SADDLE KING Western," 1970–80s. Courtesy of Voice Vintage, Daikanyama,Tokyo, Japan.

"SADDLE KING WESTERN, DIVISION OF KEY INDUSTRIES," 1970–80s. Courtesy of Funky Monkey Vintage, New Orleans, Louisiana.

SADDLEHORN Fashion Flare, 1970s. Poly/cotton blend, inexpensive tape label with content and "S" size; top edge is sewn into collar band, saving three operations. Courtesy of Nelda's Vintage, San Antonio, Texas.

"Sand and Sage WESTERN WEAR, DENVER, COLORADO," 1950. Courtesy of **The Collection of Thomas Oatman Labels.**

"SATURDAYS IN CALIFORNIA," 1980s. Including sizing and other information on label and sewing it into the collar band saves two operations. Courtesy of Nelda's Vintage, San Antonio, Texas.

"Sears WESTERN WEAR," 1970–80s. This private label has neck and sleeve sizing as part of the label.

"SHEPLERS, THE WORLD'S LARGEST WESTERN STORES," 1980s–90s. This private label was made in China and has a separate neck and sleeve size tag. Courtesy of Candy's Vintage, Boulder, Colorado.

"SING KEE, 26 BECKETT ST, SAN FRANCISCO, DRY CLEAN ONLY," 1940s. Rare, very early Western-shirt tailor label. Courtesy of the National Cowboy & Western Heritage Museum, Oklahoma City, Oklahoma.

Sport Togs by GWG, UNION LABEL, SHRUNK," 1960s. Displays an interesting selling point. Courtesy of Ronny Weiser, Las Vegas, Nevada.

"SQUARE DANCE REGISTERED DESIGNS, CREATED IN CANADA," 1950s. Courtesy of Ronny Weiser, Las Vegas, Nevada.

"STA'S WESTERN TOGS, SAN ANGELO, TEXAS," 1962. An unusual label on a shirttail. Courtesy of the National Cowboy & Western Heritage Museum, Oklahoma City, Oklahoma.

"STABLE GEAR WESTERN WEAR INC.," 1970–80s. Label is sewn into collar band.

"STIR-UPS, Western Model, MACHINE WASH WARM, TUMBLE DRY," 1970–80s. Label is side-stitched and has neck size and sleeve length and care instructions in the label. Courtesy of Full Up Vintage, Daikanyama, Tokyo, Japan.

"THE ORIGINAL SUN VALLEY, Guaranteed Washable," 1950–60s. Being washable was a big selling point. Courtesy of The Collection of Thomas Oatman Labels.

"TAILORED by Thunderbird, CHANA, NEBRASKA, PRESCOTT, ARIZONA," 1950–60s. A neck and sleeve size tag is on the side. Courtesy of Santa Monica Vintage, Tokyo, Japan.

"Tanbark," 1940s. A collar stamp (predating size tags) shows neck and sleeve size and "HAND WASH-ABLE." Courtesy of Candy's, Boulder, Colorado.

"DISTINCTIVELY DETAILED Tem-Tex, WESTERN SHIRT, STYLED IN THE HEART OF TEXAS," 1950s. Features the model name and neck and sleeve size on the collar stamp. Unusual care tag. Made by Feldt Mfg. Lined. Courtesy of Ronny Weiser, Las Vegas, Nevada.

"DISTINCTIVELY STYLED Tem-Tex, WESTERN SHIRT MADE IN THE HEART OF TEXAS," 1950s. Snap-Per-Roo tape label in collar-band seam.

"OVEN BAKED PERMANENT PRESS, Tem-Tex WESTERN Sportswear, EXTRA LONG TAILS . . .," 1950s. Features a "permanent press," neck and sleeve size collar-band stamp (predating size tags).

"DISTINCTIVE Tem-Tex, WESTERN Sportswear, EXTRA LONG TAILS," 1950s. Collar stamp predates size tags. Courtesy of Ronny Weiser, Las Vegas, Nevada.

"DISTINCTIVELY STYLED Tem-Tex, WESTERN SHIRT MADE IN THE HEART OF TEXAS," early 1950s–60s. Made by Feldt Mfg. Courtesy of Ronny Weiser, Las Vegas, Nevada.

Tem-Tex hangtag, 1950s. By Feldt Mfg., Stamford, Texas.

Reverse side of Feldt Mfg. Tem-Tex hangtag.

Tem-Tex hangtags and pen-slot tag, 1960s. This was Feldt's tag but their address changed after Karman purchased the brand in 1956. Courtesy of Ronny Weiser, Las Vegas, Nevada.

"Tem Tex WESTERN FLAIR SPORTS-WEAR," 1960–70s. Made by Karman. Note the hyphen between Tem and Tex has been dropped. Courtesy of Fine Clothing Daddy Vintage, Osaka, Japan.

"tem tex," 1980s. The label is glued, but the neck and sleeve size tag has been sewed in the collar-band seam. Courtesy of Ronny Weiser, Las Vegas, Nevada.

"Tem Tex," 1970–80s. Label is side stitched. The brand was later discontinued.

"TOM THUMB, SANFORIZED, 100% COTTON," 1950s. A variegated tape label with child's size "2" and fabric content sewn into collar band. Courtesy of Steve Weil, Denver, Colorado.

"TRAIL BOSS, Tailored Westerns," 1960s.

"TRAIL RIDGE Westerns," 1960s. The tape label is sewn into the collar band, saving operations. Ralph Barrett of Denver sold the label to Miller in the 1970s. Courtesy of Ronny Weiser, Las Vegas, Nevada.

"TRAIL RIDGE Westerns," 1962. From the Fred Mueller Catalog. Courtesy of Miller International, Denver, Colorado.

"Vaquero Fashions, TAYLOR-BERKE IN CALIFORNIA," 1940–50s. Courtesy of Ronny Weiser, Las Vegas, Nevada.

"WAGON BOSS," 1950s. "Frontier Shop" and neck and sleeve sizes are typed on the label during manufacturing.

"Walker's FT WORTH," 1950–60s. Courtesy of the National Cowboy & Western Heritage Museum, Oklahoma City, Oklahoma.

"Werstein's OF CALIFORNIA, SPORTS-WEAR," 1950s. Courtesy of the National Cowboy & Western Heritage Museum, Oklahoma City, Oklahoma.

"WESTERN CLASSICS by Guy Garrett," 1970–80s. "Made in USA" tag hangs on the side. Courtesy of Full Up Vintage, Daikanyama, Tokyo, Japan.

"WESTERN Dude," 1970–80s.

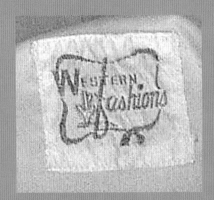

"Western fashions," 1970–80s

"WESTERN GIRL, Fishback Mfg. Co., DENVER," 1950s. The early size tag was preprinted and later stamped for style and size. Courtesy of David Little, Cody Antique Mall, Cody, Wyoming.

"Western SPORTSWEAR, WASHABLE, ALL COTTON," 1950s. Label is from a boy's wool lace-up pullover. Courtesy of Dan Shapiro, Southwest, Ltd., Costa Mesa, California.

"Westernaire by LIONDALE, SANFORIZED," 1940–50s.

"STYLED BY William Barry, WB," 1960s. From a lace-up wool pullover. Courtesy of La Rosa Vintage Boutique, San Francisco, California.

"Wolfe's Sportsmen's Headquarters, Salt Lake City," 1960s. The neck and sleeve size tag have been sewed into the neck band. Courtesy of Ronny Weiser, Las Vegas, Nevada.

"Wrangler PERMANENT PRESS, LONG TAILS, MADE IN U.S.A.," 1970–80s.

A Wrangler hangtag, 1960. Courtesy of Wrangler.

"Wrangler SANFORIZED, EXTRA LONG TAILS, MADE IN U.S.A.," 1960–70s. Courtesy of Brian Stratton, South Amboy, New Jersey.

"Wrangler," 2003. An imported shirt.

"Wyoming Woolens, BLACK SHEEP INC., Jackson Hole, WYOMING," 2000. A standard "L" size tag hangs below.

"Authentic Western Youngbloods," 1970–80s. Courtesy of Full Up Vintage, Daikanyama, Tokyo, Japan.

PART 4
Appendix

Glossary ★

appliqué: decorative trim sewn onto a garment

Bakelite: a hard, synthetic resin made from formaldehyde and phenol used in buttons, predates plastic; a brand name

bonnaz: a trim sewn down in a pattern, often soutache or floral

chenille: one of the finest forms of embroidery used in Western shirts in the 1940–50s, a heavy-coverage chain stitch that is machine sewn but maneuvered by hand, not automated. Used in decorative designs including floral and western motifs, and custom lettering, as in saddle club and bowling shirts. Expensive and requiring highly skilled workers, it is largely a lost art since the 1960s. Today, chenille embroidery on the yokes, collar, and sleeves would easily double the cost of a garment.

colorways: the combination of colors and patterns available in a given shirt design by a given manufacturer; one shirt design is frequently available in several colorways

contoured collar: a curved or shaped collar, three inches or longer, used in the 1930s–40s

contractor: an independently owned and managed factory

conventional fashion: mainstream shirt design, basic and plain with little special treatment; non-Western styling

crossover: shirt styling with both conventional and Western design elements

dobby: a type of fabric (often cotton or a blend) with a small, repeating, usually geometric, woven pattern

dog house pleat: when the end of a placket is folded to a point above a box-stitch pattern

embroidery: decorative stitching; it includes many techniques and motifs

flap pocket: a patch pocket or inside-hanging pocket with a shaped or straight flap over the top, usually secured with a button or a snap

form-fit: a shirt body cut to correspond to the shape of the physique, usually broader at the shoulders, tapering to the waist, and widening over the hips

★ ★

French front: a casual collar and front lapel treatment; collar lays flatter than constructed collar band type as it has no collar band or top center placket on shirt front; similar in construction to a suit-jacket lapel; popular during the 1940 and '50s in men's and women's sportswear and Western shirts

gabardine: a tightly woven twill weave with the rib running on the bias; often made of wool, rayon, or other heavier blends, originally intended for suiting

IR: irregular; is an imperfect factory second or has a defect

jobber: a wholesale distributor, not a manufacturer

lining: 1. an inner-lining is used to reinforce collars, cuffs, and top-center plackets so they lay more smoothly and hold snaps securely. Can be non-woven to avoid a different rate of shrinking than the outer fabric. 2. A lining, often satin, used in wool shirts as a sign of quality and to make the shirt feel smoother to the touch on the back of the neck and shoulders. Can be used on the collar band and/or inside yoke.

mother-of-pearl buttons and snaps: made of genuine natural seashell; each is unique with wavy and shimmering stripes of iridescence

mom-and-pop store: small, independent retail stores traditionally run by husband and wife, as opposed to modern big-box and chain retailers

new/old: vintage garments as new, unworn; the best examples are in factory-new condition with original hangtags and packaging

patch pocket: a pocket that has an opening at the top and is sewn on the sides and bottom over the main body of a shirt

pearl snap: a snap or button with a natural shell insert; shortened from mother-of-pearl, the smooth, pearly lining in oyster and other clam shells. Natural pearl gave way to synthetic inserts due to their tendency to crack and their higher cost. Synthetic snaps are sometimes called pearl snaps or pearl buttons, both misnomers.

★ ★

picker: a person who shops thrift stores and estate sales for vintage garments to resell to vintage stores and collectors

placket front: a top-stitched, reinforced strip of fabric on the center of a shirt. Snaps require three fabric plies so Western shirts usually have a placket front to hold the snaps securely. Early Western shirts with buttons did not require a placket.

piping: a fabric-covered cord used as decorative edging

ply: layer of fabric; e.g. the yoke is a separate ply over the body of a shirt

provenance: the history and background of an item or chain of ownership; celebrity, photography, and documentation add value

saddle stitch: a decorative stitch, often in a contrasting stitch-space-stitch pattern

sateen: a lustrous fabric designed to look and feel like satin, that is actually cotton in vintage shirts. Now, sateen is usually polyester fibers woven with fill yarns floating over warp yarns.

satin: a shiny, smooth (on one side) fabric made of silk, nylon, polyester, or rayon

"sawtooth" pocket: a pocket flap with, usually, two points in a "W" shape

shank buttons: a type of button used in Western shirts primarily from the 1930s to the 50s, characterized by a dome top and usually made of Bakelite or natural shell, with a sew-through metal stem underneath

sheeting: a plain-woven cloth available in numerous weights

sleeve placket: a reinforced strip of fabric top stitched from the cuff several inches along the sleeve opening

smile pocket: a slash opening in a variety of shapes (curved or straight) with a pocket pouch hanging on the inside of the shirt. It is often a piped opening with embroidered arrows or tabs sewn at each end.

sportswear: casual apparel with a sporty flair, not dressy or formal

★ ★

staple style: a garment style with a product cycle lasting years, not seasons

suiting: a heavy-weight garment material made for use in suits but also used in early Western shirts; often wool or rayon

two-tone: two contrasting colors, shades, or patterns in the same garment; often the yokes contrast with the body

top-stitching: a row of stitching at the edge of a seam on the face-side of fabric

Urban Cowboy: the first mass-market Western apparel movement, often characterized by flashy, flamboyant satin and fringed Western shirt styles; a term inspired by the 1978 movie *Urban Cowboy* starring John Travolta

yarn dye: usually a reference to plaid fabric with colored yarns that are dyed prior to weaving, as opposed to printed or piece-dyed fabric

yoke: a top-stitched ply of fabric covering the front or back shoulder area of a shirt; a major Western design element that comes in various pointed, scalloped, and contoured shapes to emphasize broad shoulders. Front yokes are attributed to Western shirt design; conventional and sportswear shirts may have straight back yokes, but not front yokes.

"Mayfair, Los Angeles, Beverly Hills, Hollywood," 1940s. Features chenille embroidery, piping, "V" smile pockets with sew-on tabs, very early domed snaps, a contoured collar, six-snap shotgun cuffs, and unusual tail contour. Courtesy of David Little, Cody Antique Mall, Cody, Wyoming.

★ ★

Bibliography ★★★

Delano, Sharon and David Rieff. *Texas Boots*. New York: Penguin Books, 1981.

Downey, Lynn, Jill Lynch, and Kathleen McDonough. *This Is A Pair of Levi Jeans*. San Francisco: Levi Strauss & Co. Publisher, 1995.

George-Warren, Holly and Michelle Freedman. *How the West Was Worn*. New York: Harry N. Abrams, 2001.

Glasman, Natacha. *Jeans Reference Labels Source Book*. Editions Yocar,

Greenlaw, M. Jean. *Ranch Dressing: The Story of Western Wear, Lodestar*. New York: Dutton/Penguin, 1993.

Heide, Robert and John Gilman. *Box Office Buckaroos*. New York: Cross River Press, 1989.

Kapoun, Robert W. and Charles J. Lohrmann. *Language of the Robe*. Salt Lake City: Gibbs Smith, Publisher, 1997.

Oatman, Thomas, ed. *The Collection of Thomas Oatman Labels*. Tokyo: K's & Company, 1989.

★★

Resources ★

The following is a guide to sources of genuine vintage and vintage–inspired Western shirts in the United States, Canada, Europe, and Japan. We honor those who have been in the business more than fifty years in bold lettering. As such, this is a hall of fame for stores that support the classics.

There remains a strong grassroots movement that appreciates classic Western. These people are young and old, ranchers and cowboys, musicians, truck drivers, movie costumers, and the rest of us who grew up with a love for the American West. We live everywhere: Tucson to Tokyo, Buffalo to Brussels.

The following retailers maintain the tradition. Our apologies for any omissions. Stores selling vintage-inspired shirts are listed first, those that sell actual vintage are listed next. These vintage stores helped in the research of this book.

U.S.A.

Alabama
Preston's, Athens, AL

Arizona
Saba's Western Stores
Mesa, AZ
Since 1927

Shades of the West, Inc.
Scottsdale, AZ

Rawhide Western Town
Scottsdale, AZ

Cowboy Corral
Sedona, AZ

California
Boot Barn
Locations across California:
Bakersfield, Canoga Park, Canyon Country, El Cajon, Los Alamitos, Lake Forest, Orange, Paso Robles, San Bernardino, San Diego, San Martin, Torrance, Ventura

Boot Star
West Hollywood, CA

Gene Autry Museum of Western Heritage
Los Angeles, CA

Billy Martin's
Los Angeles, CA

San Luis Obispo County
Farm Supply
Paso Robles & San Luis
Obispo, CA
Since 1950

Cabaline Saddle Shop
Point Reyes Station, CA

Jedlicka's
Santa Barbara, CA
Since 1947

Jackalope Crossing/Buckaroo
Sonoma, CA

King's
Studio City, CA
Since 1946

Country General Store
Van Nuys, CA
Since 1947

Vintage Stores:
Southwest, Ltd.
Vintage Western Wear
(dead stock)
Costa Mesa, CA

La Rosa Vintage Boutique
San Francisco, CA

Aaardvark's Odd Ark
San Francisco, CA

Play Clothes Vintage
Studio City, CA

Colorado
Rockmount Ranch Wear
Denver, CO
Since 1946

Cry Baby Ranch
Denver, CO

Kemo Sabe
Aspen, CO

Brok'n Spoke
Colorado Springs, CO

Stage Western
Estes Park, CO

Appaloosa Trading Co.
Durango, CO

FM Light
Steamboat Springs, CO
Since 1905

Soda Creek Outfitter
Steamboat Springs, CO

Into The West
Steamboat Springs, CO

Gore Range Mountain Works
Vail, CO

Vintage Stores:
Candy's Vintage Clothing
Boulder, CO

Crown Mercantile/Ace Dry
Goods
Denver, CO

Boss Unlimited
Denver, CO

Florida
Byrd's Western Store
West Melbourne, FL

West of Old England
Stuart, FL

Georgia
Timpson Creek Gallery
Clayton, GA

Horse Town Western Store
Marietta, GA

Stampede Western Wear
Savannah, GA

Hawaii
Paniolo Trading, Inc.
Honolulu, HI

Western Classics
Honolulu, HI

Out of the West
Honolulu, HI

Circle A Western Wear, California, men's wool gaberdine embroidery, 1940s. A defunct label featuring fine chenille embroidery, smile pockets with embroidered arrows, piping, shotgun cuffs, and enamel snaps. Courtesy of David Little, Cody Antique Mall, Cody, Wyoming.

★★

Vintage Stores:
Island Treasures Antique Mall
Waikiki, HI

Bailey's
Honolulu, HI

Illinois
Alcala's
Chicago, IL

Boot Corral
Gurnee, IL
Since 1948

Louisiana
Vintage Stores:
Funky Monkey
New Orleans, LA

Miss Claudia's Vintage
Clothing & Costumes
New Orleans, LA

Maryland
Carol's Western Wear
Glen Burnie, MD

Massachusetts
Helen's Leather
Boston, MA

Rick Walker's
Boston, MA

Michigan
Scott Colburn Saddlery
Livonia, MI
Since 1951

Vintage Stores:
Cat's Meow
Royal Oaks, MI

Minnesota
RCC Western Store
Bloomington, MN
Since 1948

Mississippi
Cowboy Corner
Southaven, MS

Montana
Ranch Outfitters
Billings, MT
Since 1919

Nebraska
Wolf Bros.
Omaha, NE
Since 1945

Nevada
Boot Barn
Las Vegas, NV

New Mexico
Covered Wagon
Albuquerque, NM
Since 1949

Burro Street Clothier
Cloudcroft, NM

Nathalie's
Santa Fe, NM

Taos Cowboy
Taos, NM

New York
Lawanna's
Brooklyn, NY

East Coast Cowboy
East Hampton, NY

Billy Martin's
New York, NY

Whiskey Dust
New York, NY

Vintage Stores:

What Comes Around
Goes Around
New York, NY

Whiskey Dust
New York, NY

North Carolina
Watsonatta Western World
Boone, NC

★★★★★★★★★★★★★★★★★★★★★★★★★★★★★★★★★★★★★★

Oklahoma

The National Cowboy and
Western Heritage Museum
Oklahoma City, OK

Pennsylvania

Tepee Town
Bartonsville, PA

Lowry's Western Shop
Washington, PA

South Carolina

Pistol Creek
West Columbia and
Greenville, SC

South Dakota

Wall Drug
Wall, SD
Since 1931

Tennessee

Hewlett and Dunn
Collierville, TN

The Cowboy Store
Franklin, TN

Boot Corral
Goodlettsville, TN
Since 1948

Ranch Dressing
Nashville, TN

Texas

Black Mail
Austin, TX

ML Leddys
Fort Worth, TX
Since 1921

Luskeys/Ryons
Western Stores
Fort Worth and Weatherford,
TX
Since 1919

Maverick Saloon
and Trading Post
Fort Worth, TX

Leddy's Ranch
Fort Worth, TX
Since 1923

Pinto Ranch
Houston, TX

Crazy Ranch Designs
Houston, TX

Romancing the Range
Houston, TX

Wyoming

Ranch Outfitters
Casper, WY
Since 1919

The Wrangler/Corral West
Cheyenne, WY, and locations
throughout the West
Since 1943

Cowgirls of the West Museum
Cheyenne, WY

Buffalo Bill
Historical Center Museum
Cody, WY

Jackson Hole Clothiers
Jackson, WY

Cowboy Shop
Pinedale, WY
Since 1947

Vintage Stores:
Traditions West Antique Mall
Cody, WY

Willow Springs Antique Mall
Cody, WY

Cowboy Story Land and
Cattle Co.
Cody, WY

★ ★

Canada, Europe, and Asia:

Canada
Riley and McCormick
Calgary, AB
Canada
Since 1901

Belgium
Western Shop
Brussels

France
El Paso Booty
Paris

Western Store
Cuges Les Pins

Germany
Lucky Star Western
Berlin

Italy
Jalisco Due
Reggio Emilia

Mex 307
Torino

Norway
Los Lobos A/S
Oslo

Sweden
Kulan Trading
Hillerstorp

High Chaparral
Hillerstorp

Blue Corner
Lottorp

Tumbleweed
Vallentuna

Switzerland
VMC Jeans and Sportswear
Zurich (new and vintage)

Japan
FUNNY
Otaru, Hokkaido

America-ya
Fukuoka City, Fukuoka

Iwakyu-Horikoshi
Fukuoka City, Fukuoka

B G House
Fukuoka City, Fukuoka

Magic
Yamakado, Fukuoka

Something
Karatsu, Saga

Jeans Factory
Kochi

Cactus Blues/Johnny Angel
Kitahorie, Osaka

FUNNY Hep Navio,
IMP and Big Step,
Osaka

Nylon, Shinsaibashi
Osaka

Tokyo Disney Western Shop
Saitama

Gimick
Takamatsu

Ships
Tokyo, and locations
across Japan

Labrador Retriever
Tokyo

Backdrop
Tokyo

Slap Shot
Tokyo

Uncut Bound
Tokyo

Beaver Ueno
Tokyo

Spiritual Lab
Tokyo

FUNNY
Ikspiari, Urayasu, and Chiba

FUNNY
Yatsugatake, Kitakoma, and
Yamanashi

Favor
Yamagata

Hanger Market
Yanagawa, Fukuoka

Vintage Stores:
Hex Hiue
Nara

Fine Clothing Daddy,
Rag Up Co.
Higashi Shinsaibashi,
Chuo, Osaka

Happy Days
Nishiku, Osaka

Junk Used Clothing Shop
Mishishinsaibashi, Osaka

Pigsty Used Clothing
Higashi Shinsaibashi,
Chuo, Osaka

Full Up Used Clothing and
Goods
Daikanyama, Tokyo

Santa Monica
Harajuku, Shibuya, Laforet,
Yuhodo, and Kichijoji

Scream
Daikanyama, Tokyo

Voice Daikanyama
Shibuya, Tokyo

Singapore

Jr. Texas
Singapore

Overleaf: Prior, Denver, men's two-toned wool gaberdine, 1950s. Features a lined inside yoke, smile pockets with sew-on tabs, floral embroidery, shotgun cuffs, synthetic snaps, and a size stamp on the tail. Courtesy of Ronnie Weiser, Las Vegas, Nevada.

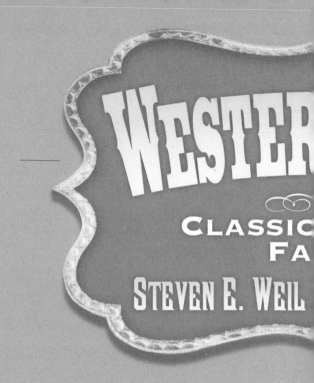

WESTER

CLASSIC
FA

STEVEN E. WEIL

1853
Levi Strauss
& Co. estab-
lished as a
dry-goods
jobber

1890s
First work
shirts made

1930s
Early
transitional
sportswear/
Western
shirts made
with buttons

1897
Tailored by
Christianfeld
established
as a pants
maker

1940s
H Bar C
California
Ranchwear
established

1999
H Bar C
California
Ranchwear
defunct

1905
Wrangler
brand used
briefly in
work wear

1947
Wrangler
brand is
revived for
jeans and
work shirts

1909
First
Pendleton
blanket
made

1912
Pendleton
begins mak-
ing clothing

1930s
Early
transitional
sportswear/
Western
shirts made
with buttons